CW00433706

OLD HITCHIN

Church Gates *c.*1905

OLD HITCHIN

Portrait of an English Market Town
from the cameras of T.B. Latchmore and others

Commentary by
Alan Fleck and Helen Poole

Phillimore

1999

Published by
PHILLIMORE & CO. LTD.
Shopwyke Manor Barn, Chichester, West Sussex

© North Hertfordshire District Council, 1999

ISBN 1 86077 109 2

Printed and bound in Great Britain by
BIDDLES LTD.
Guildford, Surrey

Contents

Thomas Benwell Latchmore (1832-1908), probably a self-portrait

Introduction

Writing a quarter of a century after contributing to the first edition, I make no apology for leaving Mary Gadd's elegant introduction untouched: it is as true now as it was then.

I have however taken the opportunity to provide an additional short chapter, drawing on William Ranger's *Report to the General Board of Health on a Preliminary Enquiry into the Sewerage, Drainage and Supply of Water and the Sanitary Condition of the Inhabitants of the Town of Hitchin*, published by HMSO in 1849, to give a snapshot of the conditions then prevalent in the town. It is easy to see the past as 'good old days'; even the recognition that disease was prevalent and death commonplace leaves one unprepared for the horrors which Ranger reveals.

★★★★

Hitchin is a thriving market town, only 35 miles north of London, in a predominantly rural area administered by the North Hertfordshire District Council, with an estimated population of around 33,000 in 1999. The Council for British Archaeology include Hitchin in their list of those towns having historic town centres of regional importance which it is essential to conserve. In 1974, the Department of the Environment, on the advice of the Historic Buildings Council, accepted that the Hitchin conservation area is one of outstanding architectural and historic interest. This official recognition served to confirm the convictions, long held by generations of its inhabitants, that their town is 'special'. Having lived here for 10 years, I admit to sharing their bias.

The production of this book happens to coincide with a national awakening of interest in the history of photography and the appreciation of photography as an art form. The spate of books of old photographs reflects a current trend for nostalgia but has also enabled the general public to appreciate a fact which has long been recognised by the historian. A good collection of photographs forms an invaluable historical record and provides a most pleasant and palatable method of absorbing a great deal of information. Hitchin is fortunate indeed to have such an important source. There are over 2,000 views of the town and portraits of Hitchin people in the museum collections, mostly taken prior to 1920. The majority of photographs in the collections and those reproduced here represent the work of a father and son, both of whom were born and died in Hitchin.

Thomas Benwell Latchmore (1832-1908) was the eldest son of a Quaker family who ran a grocery business in the High Street. He was educated at Isaac Brown and Benjamin Abbott's Academies in Hitchin and then at Ackworth, the Quaker school in Yorkshire. At first he assisted his father but an interest in chemistry led him to study photography. About 1865 he built a studio in Bancroft and set up in business. He had experimented with daguerreotypes and the collodion process but after 1871 successfully adopted the use of the dry plate method. His business thrived and enabled him in 1870 to buy out an earlier photographer, George Avery, who had worked from the Old Town Hall yard in Brand Street. 'On their completion, he moved into more commodious premises with a studio on the roof' and resided at No.11 Brand Street until his death.

He was a keen naturalist and enthusiastic cyclist. His obituary mentions the fact that he had been known to ride to London and back on his 'boneshaker' machine. He was very familiar with his town and the surrounding countryside and villages and used his camera to record them for his own interest as well as for business purposes. The majority of the photographs selected for this book are dated between 1870 and 1890 so it is reasonable to assume that they represent the work of the father, since his son was not born until 1882.

Thomas William Latchmore (1882-1946), educated at Hitchin Grammar School and Ackworth, went into partnership with his father and succeeded him in 1908 having 'already won the confidence and esteem of his fellow townsmen'. He opened a new branch in Letchworth in 1914, which was taken over from a Mr. Salter. The son inherited his father's love of Hitchin and Hertfordshire countryside but preferred to explore it on foot with his dog, Spot. He remained a bachelor, experimented with early colour photography and devoted much of his spare time to the study of archaeology, coins and local history. His house in Brand Street was over-flowing with books and papers and he was a popular lecturer. Although he died many years ago, he is still remembered with affection in Hitchin.

His interest in local history undoubtedly made him well aware of the importance of the photographic record which he and his father had created. So it is a tragedy that at his death, most of the original glass plates used by the firm seem to have been destroyed, and four of his personally annotated volumes of photographs disappeared. This loss has meant that comparatively few of the photographs in the museum collections can be given definite dates or attributions. (In this book, the work of the Latchmores that can only be attributed to the firm is marked by an asterisk at the end of the caption.) It is just possible that more of the original plates and, in particular, T.W. Latchmore's personal volumes survive. William Dunnage's manuscript history of Hitchin was rediscovered recently, having been mislaid for 20 years, so that we have not given up hope that the equally invaluable missing links in the photographic records of the town will yet be found.

Although the work of the Latchmores predominates, other photographers are represented in this book. George Avery, probably the earliest commercial photographer in Hitchin, has been mentioned and details of the career of Henry George Moulden (1861-1916) are referred to in the text. Views of the town, produced as postcards by the well-known Francis Frith (1822-98) of Reigate, who, like the Latchmores, was also a Quaker, have been included, together with scenes and portraits by other less important local men.

At this point, I should perhaps say something of how the photographs were selected from what proved to be almost an embarrassment of riches. The basis of the choice was subject interest and reprographic qualities and a great deal of heart searching was caused as the compilers realised how much would have to be omitted. This applies in particular to the section on local people because there are so many splendid carte-de-visite and studio portraits available. It was decided not to restrict the selection by date, so whilst the earliest, that of the Shambles in the old Market Place, is c.1854, the most recent are of Perks and Llewellyn in the 1950s.

Although the main purpose of this book is to present a selection of the photographic records that are available, it has also been our intention to provide in the text an introduction to the more recent history of the town. Hitchin is well endowed with documentary evidence, which has been used extensively in the county histories and by local historians such as Frederic Seebohm and, not least, in the thousands of pages of material produced by that indefatigable pioneer author of local history studies, Reginald Hine. In a sense, the existence of this large body of published work has inhibited more recent historians but there is still a great deal to be done, questions to be answered and some inaccuracies to be corrected. For instance, it is a commonly held view that the railway station was built a mile away from the centre of the town because of the opposition of leading members of the Quaker community. In fact, it was probably Lord Dacre who exerted most influence in the choice of location. In the interests of brevity and clarity many over-simplifications and bald statements have had to be made. We hope that this book may encourage people to want to find out more about the town from other sources that are available. It is not accidental that there is very little about the fine parish church or the Priory and the Radcliffe family. Many photographs exist but the buildings have not changed recently and their history has already been covered in great detail.

For convenience, the photographs have been grouped under specific headings but the overlapping of subject matter in the text serves to reflect the interdependence of all sections of a community. This book is intended to give many people a great deal of pleasure because the photographs are fascinating but it should also cause sorrow to see what has been lost. Before the earliest photograph of Hitchin, the mediaeval town was virtually intact and compact, although its buildings had already been altered many times as tastes and standards changed. The central medieval street plan still survives, but after 1850 many of the more prosperous members of the community began to desert the town centre and build imposing villas on the surrounding hillsides. New building developments extended in the direction of the station but it is in the 20th century that the housing estates have covered the ancient open field system of the royal manor of Hitchin which had supported the medieval community.

It is the scale of change which is frightening to contemplate. We accept the need for decent housing to accommodate the increased population, new industry and shops to provide prosperity and employment and that some surgery is necessary to break the stranglehold of traffic. We are thankful that the town still contains remarkably fine buildings and that modern concepts of planning and legislation provide them with some measure of statutory protection, but in the long run it must be the townspeople who decide what is important. Hitchin is typical of many English country towns but it will remain 'special' just so long as the people who live there care enough to think that it is so.

FRANCES M. GADD
Director, North Hertfordshire Museums

Wherever known, the photographers' names are given in the illustration captions. An asterisk against Latchmore's name indicates that the evidence for his being the photographer is strong but not certain.

Acknowledgements

The Hitchin Museum and the Authors would like to acknowledge the help of the following people who have kindly lent photographs or confirmed details of information: Caldicott School; *Chemist and Druggist*; Mr. A.B. Curry; Mr. A.M. Foster; Mr. G.A. Day, Markets Superintendent; Mr. P. Day of Newtons; Miss E.A. Latchmore; Miss V.E. Lewis; William Ransom & Son Ltd.; G.W. Russell & Son Ltd.; Mr. B. Sanders; and Mr. G. Thomson.

Townscape

The churchyard served early Hitchin as an area where children could play, sheep could graze, women could hang washing, and, in the medieval French wars, where troops could muster. There was also, more secretly, some bodysnatching, and a case in 1825 led to a move to erect fencing, which was completed in 1828, thanks to the efforts of H.S. Merrett, the surveyor, and his apprentice George Beaver, with over £500 from public subscriptions.

The corner shop, then a butcher's, was later George Savage's, a tailor and woollen draper who shared premises in 1903 with H.G. Moulden, one of the men to whom this book is indebted. Moulden opened a Photo Studio near the Biggin in 1885, after training under Latchmore and at Bedford; two moves later, he set up in 1904 in High Street as photographer and musical dealer. In the 1890s he became St Mary's Church organist, and an FRCO.

Next door was the milliner Mrs. Martha Flint, 'the noted house for Sailor Hats' in an 1897 advertisement, who had materials and hats of all kinds. Halseys were at 12 Market Place, as grocers, tea dealers and provision merchants.

Soon after the churchyard was fenced in, the Brand Street/Bedford Road area began to change character. One photo shows part of the Quaker Meeting House, built in 1840 on Pound Farm Yard, and across Grammar School Walk, on the site of the new Town Hall, are buildings such as Dr. Oswald Foster's premises.

Nearby, the hospital went up in 1840 with 16 beds to cater for those whom it was difficult or dangerous to move after accidents, and those worried about being distanced from their families, which the earlier system had not been able to manage. It was built at a cost of £4,931 on meadow land bought from Thomas Wilshere, and now, with Hampden House which is also in the photo, it forms part of the local Health Authority's establishment.

1 (left) Church Gates, *c.*1903 *Francis Frith & Co., Reigate*

2 Grammar School Walk and the old Quaker Meeting House, before 1900 *Latchmore*

3 Bedford Road and the Infirmary, 1895 *Latchmore*

1

4 Biggin Lane with Mrs. Albert Masters, 1930 *F. Sharp of Highbury*

5 Hollow Lane looking towards the town *Latchmore*

The Biggin Lane picture shows two buildings now gone, the one on the left being part of St Andrew's School, called St Mary's when it was built in 1854, and demolished in 1971 for the new market. The other lost building was a shoe maker's, Spencer, whose ghostly shape survives in the brickwork of Warner's Almshouses next door. These were rebuilt by Daniel Warner 'for the warmer and better comfort of the poorest widows or ancient couples in this town' with a grant from Elizabeth Lucas's legacies for the poor of Hitchin, and the same source provided funds to enlarge the building in 1893. By this time, 1930, the almshouses consisted of six

6 High Street, before 1900 *Latchmore*

tenements for six women who received a weekly allowance which varied from 3s. 6d. to 6s.

On the other side of Queen Street, Hollow Lane exhibits a distinctly rural appearance, looking down into the town past what is now Garrison Court. The path to the left led up to the Cemetery where the chapel was consecrated in April 1857, but it was not connected to the town by road until 1874, after people wrote in complaint to the local paper.

In *An Artist Looks at Hitchin*, the locally born artist F.L. Griggs (1876-1938) mentions a walk in which 'we start by Biggin Lane, cross Queen Street, and enter an alley and steeply ascending path', and the third view shows his parents' shop, a pastry cook and confectioner's on High Street. Griggs loved Hitchin and said: 'I sincerely believe it to have been one of the most beautiful small towns of England, set in one of her happiest counties.' He attempted to immortalise the town of his birth in a series of six etchings done in Bridge Street in 1897, after he had left his attic studio at 22 High Street, and he would often return to Hitchin in later years.

Beyond the Griggs's shop cluster a group of three pubs: *The Black Horse*, *The White Horse* and *The Three Horseshoes*, each of which sold a different local brew—Fordhams of Ashwell, McMullens of Hertford, and Royston & Stout. Beyond was Drake's

7 Bancroft looking towards Moss's Corner, *c.*1866 *Latchmore*

the clothier, and No.14 was the site of Dr. Frederick Hawkins's first Hitchin Dispensary, which opened in 1823—a move which culminated in the Hitchin Hospital.

Griggs claimed that Bancroft was one of the most beautiful streets in England, with its gently curved length full of gracious buildings. Its charm is enhanced by the sight of these schoolgirls, outside what used to be Nicholls, in appropriate versions of the then fashionable crinoline. The dominating feature is, however, Moss's Corner, though it was still then yet another pub—*The Trooper*, run by the landlord John Carter. John Moss had started in Bancroft in 1859, at a rent of £29 a year, in premises later occupied by the police station. The first week's takings were 30s., but 40 years later the firm had over thirty employees, and by 1918 it had 10 town and district branches, being the largest provision shop that Hitchin had ever produced. W.B. Moss took over from his father in 1868, and although he was responsible for the expansion of the firm, and had warehouses built on Portmill Lane, he still found time to be a Wesleyan minister and Hitchin councillor.

8 Bridge Street, *c.*1905   *Latchmore*

The first point of interest in this scene is the board warning that the bridge is not safe for traction engines or other heavy traffic, dating from the days before it was strengthened. Beyond *The Plough*, two pigs hang drying in the sun, outside the splendid old building which the Crawley family ran as a butcher's shop from the 1870s, and one can also see part of Mr. Burrows's upholstery business. Further up, on Tilehouse Street is the music shop run by a well-known local figure, Bradly Gatward, who was a member of the family who started as jewellers in

Hitchin Market Place in 1760. His over riding interest was music, and he spent over seventy years as organist and choir master, chiefly at Tilehouse Street Baptist Church.

This love of music led him to open showrooms, first in Sun Street, and then in the premises shown here where he displayed pianos and other musical instruments. He was also an authority on old china, adding a china department to the main shop, and he had earlier been known as a fine local sportsman, and after this very full life, he died at the age of 90 in 1947.

9 Tilehouse Street, *c.*1892 *Latchmore*

10 Tilehouse Street, opposite *The Highlander*, between 1884 and 1907 *Latchmore*

Towards the top of Tilehouse Street we find a similar pattern of trade to that in Bridge Street, with a butcher, James Cooper, and the inevitable representation of pubs. The superb old building of the *Cooper's Arms* was then in the care of Jack Webb, who also hired out horses, carriages and traps, while across the road stood the domain of John Anderson, who for a short time in the early 1890s functioned as a beer retailer and bill poster from this shop.

Quite a bit of bill posting can be seen on the shed opposite the nearby *Highlander* pub, where there are advertisements for 'Amateur Gardening', various railway excursions and an exhibition at Sandy which was organised by Major Shuttleworth of Old Warden. It was his son whose contribution to flying was commemorated in the Shuttleworth Collection.

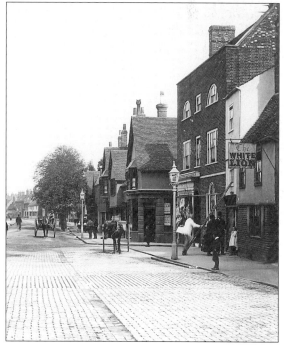

11 Bancroft and the entrance to Portmill Lane, *c.*1896 *Latchmore*

Advertising also figures in Jackson's window in Bancroft, for the sale of farm implements, cart horses and cows. Across Portmill Lane, cows are for sale in a different form, outside Ansell's the butchers.

12 High Street looking towards the corn exchange, between 1882 and 1898 *Latchmore*

13 High Street, between 1902 and 1921 *Francis Frith and Co.*

14 Bancroft and the entrance to Hermitage Road, 1929 *Latchmore*

15 High Street looking towards Bancroft, between 1867 and 1878 *Latchmore*

Like many old streets, Bancroft was affected by the advent of the supermarket type of shop, and one result was the demolition of the old property to the right of Hermitage Road. One of these listed buildings was a 15th-century hall house with 17th-century gables, which had probably been the home of a wealthy wool merchant. Latterly it formed the joinery Works of P.H. Barker & Son, but when the buildings went in 1958, it proved impossible to retain any of the old walls. Now, the only timber framing in that area is on the two 20th-century buildings by Hermitage Road.

High Street too has altered, for instance when Woolworths moved in the 1930s to where Boots now is, and later in 1964 when Perks and Llewellyn came down to make way for a larger Woolworths. In the middle of this stood *The Cock Hotel* after which the street was named, and where cock-fights took place. Originating in the 15th century, it was the main inn for market traders, and in the 18th century vestry meetings were held there. In the 19th century, it stocked Pryor, Reid & Co.'s ale, yet another variety for local drinkers.

Like the Pryors, the people who rebuilt the bank were also Quakers. In 1841, when Piersons Bank failed, the site was bought by Sharples, Exton and Lucas who later erected the building which now houses Barclays Bank. They had earlier been across the road at No.25, next door to the grocery business of Frank Latchmore, brother to T.B. to whom this book owes its life. T.B. had helped his father in that shop before moving to open a photography shop in Bancroft in 1865. His portrait appears on page vi.

Nearby was a famous Hitchin landmark, the clock made by Robert Street, watchmaker, silversmith and jeweller on High Street. He also ran a farm at Wellbury and was involved in local government as manager of the town's water supply for 15 years. He was a Low Churchman, and when Canon Hensley had the choirboys turning east for the Creed, Street turned west, to his neighbours' surprise.

16 Sun Street looking towards Market Place, *c*.1900 *Latchmore*

17   Bancroft and the Skynners Almshouses, *c.*1900   *Latchmore*

In 1733 Thomas Paternoster, a stationer of Hitchin, was indicted for placing a cartload of fire-wood in Angel Street and obstructing the highway, and this gives some indication of how long the Paternoster family had been connected with Hitchin before the time of this picture. The street originally took its name from the famous old pub, *The Angel Vaults*, demolished in 1956, and after a short spell when it was known as St Mary Street, Sun Street was the accepted name. The Paternosters persisted, under the Printing Office sign whence issued various items, from election posters to the *Hitchin Advertiser*, edited by Charles Paternoster. His niece Sarah ran the stationery and bookselling business which amal-gamated with Charles Hales, with premises in Market Square; but Sun Street had other specialities. At one time, the family ran a music selling business, and in 1865, the Paternoster's First-Class Subscription Library and Reading Rooms could offer Hitchin people 5,000 volumes to choose from, plus local papers and magazines, a vital part of life before the introduction of our present public library system.

More fundamental needs were catered for on Sun Street by another of Hitchin's important families, the Lucases, whose brewery looms up on the far right of the scene. This has now gone, but the original building had leads on the roof carrying the date of 1771. William Lucas's marriage settlement in 1783 mentions that the site contained his house and associated outbuildings right down as far as the river where they caused some obstruction. Matilda Lucas recalled that in her mid-19th-century childhood, 'the brewery garden went to the Swimming Bath and then right away to Queen Street. Through a malting you could get into Bridge Street. There was no

18   London Road and the entrance to Gosmore Road   *Latchmore*

19 Bedford Road, *c*.1900 *Latchmore*

limit to the fruit grown and eaten by us in that garden.' To keep this going, a writer in 1907 says that Lucases' bottled beer was allowed to mature naturally in the bottle, with no artificial carbonation, and on the site they also had a mineral water factory, cooperage, cask and bottle-washing departments and carpenters' and engineers' shops, so it must have been almost self-sufficient.

Brewing and its allied trades were vital to Hitchin, and one of the buildings by the Almshouses on Bancroft had been a malthouse, though by the time of this photograph it was a private house. The Almshouses date from the benefactions of John Skynner and his son Ralph in 1666 and 1696, catering for 16 married couples. This meant that at one time Hitchin had more foundations of almshouses than any other place in the county.

At this time, Phillips had premises on both sides of Bancroft, the other being the Manor House where they started in the 1880s. Further down, where Regal Chambers now stands, there was a dairy farm. About 1900 Arthur Ransom ran it as a dairy and stud farm, but a big fire killed his pigs and roasted the fowls who used to roost in the trees around. The buildings were not seriously damaged and it soon became the head-quarters of the Wallace Dairies.

The London Road scene also exhibits a quiet rural air and is little changed, except for the maintenance of the roadside verges and the more peaceful traffic. The uniformed girls perch precariously on the slope by the turning off to Gosmore, and it is interesting to note that most of them are wearing hats, which their modern counterparts would not tolerate. Many are straw hats which may well have come from the Luton factories which influenced life here so much.

Bedford Road too had its share of horse-drawn transport to give the picture a suitably tranquil air. Here we see a cart bearing the board of George Parker who, at the turn of the century, was running *The Woolpack* public house at Starlings Bridge, as well as the business of furniture remover and timber and carting contractor. The fountain at which this hard-working animal is refreshing itself was erected in 1887 by the executors of Joseph Sharples, a prominent member of the Quaker family who started the Hitchin bank which eventually became part of Barclays. His drinking fountain has been less fortunate in its protectors as it now lies sadly in a car park not far from its original site. The large house on the corner of Oughton Head Way once belonged to W.B. Moss.

20   Bridge Street between 1882 and 1895   *Latchmore*

Bridge Street here shows plenty of variety, from Henry Waller the rope maker, beside the Brewery wall, to *The Dial* pub, then run by Herbert Crawley who was also a butcher. By 1904 *The Plough* had appeared, and a few years later the title became *The Plough and Dial*, which remained until its closure in 1966.

Up the road were Odells, carriage-building brothers whose father was a shoeing smith by examination at 32 Bridge Street. These buildings had been part of the old Priory, with late 16th-century additions by the ford where the bridge is now. In 1914 James Fordham moved there, though still retaining his Park Street forge, and despite the difficulties from competition with cars, he remained there till 1925.

Then Percy Webb set up as an agricultural engineer there, but by 1970 the only inhabitant was an old horse which drew the scrap dealer's cart. By this time the house was badly in need of the repair it received when it became architects' offices and was given a Civic Trust Award in 1972.

The view down Bucklersbury begins at the Shop of Mr. Charles Hales who came to Hitchin and bought Messrs. Pain and Brook's booksellers' business in 1869. Three years later, Mr. Paternoster left his family business at Sun Street, leaving the management side to his niece Sarah, and she went into partnership with Mr. Hales. This continued successfully until her death in 1901. After this Hales continued with some fifty assistants in the different departments of

21 Bucklersbury from the Market Place, 1869-72 *Latchmore*

his business, and had seven machines running in the Printing Works. He died in 1906, but the name of Paternoster and Hales carried on for many long years, both here and at 27 Sun Street.

Down the street was *The George*, then providing Steeds Ales of Baldock, and across the road was one of Hitchin's most important buildings, the pawnbroker's shop. People would go in on Monday with the suits they had worn on the Sunday, pawn them for about 18d., and hope to redeem them on the following Saturday. It was run by Frederick Morley and lasted into the 1940s.

22   Paynes Park and Old Park Road before 1895   *Latchmore*

Very little remains of this view of the Old Park Road corner, the only survivor being the building in the background. This was then *The Swan with Two Necks*, demolished to make way for the Tilehouse Street relief road, together with the buildings to its right. Furthest right was *The Waggon and Horses*, which though closing in 1972 survived until 1982.

On the left, with the intriguing notice about the Fire Brigade, is part of the Old Free School, also demolished for road-widening, in 1949. Now the Hine Memorial Garden, tablets set in the wall remind one of its earlier history. The early benefactors are named, and Ralph Skynner noted that in 1678 he had finished the Free School which was begun in 1640 by voluntary contributions.

When the new Grammar School buildings were officially opened in 1891, Mr. Tuke commented that if the founders Mattock and Kemp could see the result of their donation of a few acres of land and a small house in Tilers Street, they would be filled with wonder and admiration. That small house too had been a school before being superseded in

1640, so knowledge must have been imparted on that site for over 300 years.

The main feature of the view from Windmill Hill is the abundance of trees, especially in the area around the church where they provide almost total cover in what is now a collection of car parks and open spaces. On the right of the large tree in the foreground can be seen the old Market Place, in which the sign of Timothy Whites the chemists can just be seen beside the Corn Exchange. Nearer the camera, in amongst a fascinating cluster of roofs, can be made out the patterned brickwork of the old school by the church, demolished as part of the new Market scheme.

The view was taken high up on Windmill Hill which takes its name from a mid-18th-century windmill built there by Joseph Ransom, then a baker in Hitchin. His son John added Grove Mill to the family properties, and John's son Joshua tried to set up machinery for throwing silk at Grove Mill, though this failed. Joshua became involved in great legal wrangles over Grove Mill and eventually left the area, but the windmill on

23   View of Hitchin from Windmill Hill, 1927   *Latchmore*

Windmill Hill came to a very dramatic end. It had always been a well-known landmark in the town as it stood so well, and there were tales told about one of the millers there who was so strong that he could carry three cwt. loads of wheat under each arm up the massive steps of the mill. It was a post mill, on a pivot so that a horse had to be borrowed to adjust the top to the wind, and this proved to be its downfall. One weekend in November 1875, a storm blew up and as the canvas sails had not been set correctly, they revolved too rapidly and caused overheating which set the windmill alight. The fire brigade arrived and put out this early fire with their handpump, and then left, with the fire apparently under control. It caught alight again, however, and this time it proved impossible to stop. The wind was so strong that the fire brigade could no longer play their hoses on the fire, and so concentrated on saving some of the large timbers. Firemen were on duty from 7.15a.m. to 9.45p.m. to keep a watch on the state of the building and to protect the public, many of whom came up the hill to see the last hours of the mill.

24   View from the path beside the Dell, Windmill Hill   *Latchmore*

In 1880 Frederic Seebohm made a tunnel under Walsworth Road, the first of many in that area. This one led from his garden in Hermitage Road to the plantation opposite, called the Dell, beside which the first picture was taken, and where the Woodside Open Air Theatre was opened in 1951. The Seebohm involvement in this part of Hitchin was very strong and persisted until 1919 when Seebohm's daughters gave the lower part of Windmill Hill to the town as an interesting playground site. At this time, the War Memorial Committee decided to

recommend the site as a suitable place for the town's monument to those who fell in the First World War. Another idea suggested a recreation ground as a second memorial scheme, on the south side of the hill on land near Hollow Lane which belonged to Miss Wilshere, whose family had also played a vital role in the formation of Hitchin.

In 1874 Frederic Seebohm made a free gift of land from his Hermitage estate to the Local Board, to improve access to the station from Bancroft. This road was officially opened in July 1875, with over 1,000 people there to cheer Seebohm and his fellow-Quaker J.H. Tuke for making the road possible. At this time some of the lovely old box trees were cut down, but others stayed, until in 1919 it was decided that the remainder should go. This was after a great storm in the previous year had brought down one of these trees and it was argued that although they were held in place by chains and stanchions, they were no longer safe. Reginald Hine wrote a piteous letter to the *Express* in which he said that the trees dated from Edward IV's reign when they were planted as a box-edging to the garden for those living at the new Brotherhood House in Bancroft. Box trees were also planted locally as they could be used for hat blocks in the all-important Luton factories, but although Hine pointed out that in Edward IV's time, a local

25   Hermitage Road after 1875   *Latchmore*

26 St Andrew's Place
W. & L. Lewes?

man had been hanged for felling a tree in the covers of Hitch Wood, the Hermitage Road box trees were felled. They were not totally forgotten, as Mr. Barker presented the successors of the Local Board, Hitchin Urban District Council, with a gavel and block made from some of the old wood.

At the same time as houses were being built along the north side of Hermitage Road, the way of life of a large part of Hitchin's community was undergoing an even more far-reaching change, with the demolition of the houses round Queen Street in the late 1920s. The whole area had always had something of a reputation as rather unhealthy, which occasional forays by Medical Officers did nothing to disprove. The attitude of the establishment to the kind of area shown in the picture of St Andrew's Place comes out in the foundation records of the nearby St Andrew's School which was set up for the instruction of the very lowest classes 'and the only way to secure their attendance is by building a schoolroom in the midst of them.' As the parents of children likely to go to this school relied on income from their children's straw plaiting, this activity formed part of the school's daily routine, until the 1870 Education Act put an end to it.

On the other side of Queen Street, also partly demolished in the 1920s, was Portmill Lane whose name commemorates the old watermill which came to the end of a long life as a result of a health inspector's report in 1850. He recommended its demolition as part of a scheme to clean up the river, and the Local Board bought Port Mill in 1850. It had been a source of nuisance for many

years, as for instance in 1718 when William Haynes was indicted for obstructing the water flowing to his corn mill, Port Mill, and causing it to overflow into the highway. The mill went in 1852 and George Beaver put up plans for a new bridge in Portmill Lane for the passage of river water and sewage mains, but by 1857 houses along the Hiz in Bridge Street and Portmill Lane flooded knee-deep after a violent storm.

Eventually, such problems became a thing of the past when the whole aspect of that part of the town was radically altered in one of the Council's most dramatic actions. In the area including St Andrews Street, Queen Street and Portmill Lane, 174 houses were demolished in the late 1920s, and 637 people were rehoused, largely on the Sunnyside estate. Crown Yard with its ageing houses made way for a car park.

27 Crown Yard, Portmill Lane, before 1927 *W. & L. Lewes of Hitchin*

28   Market Place and the Shambles, 1856   *Latchmore*

29   Market Place and the Shambles, 1854

William Lucas's Journal for April 1854 noted: 'A subscription is set on foot towards pulling down the houses in the Market Place which now stand in front of the new Corn Exchange. £1,600 or more is required, a large sum certainly for a mere local improvement.' The houses he referred to can be seen here in photographs from the first stages of the process. The upper one is said to be copied from a daguerreotype, a process which involved putting the image straight on to a sensitised silvered copper plate and then subjecting it to mercury fumes. This meant that only one image could be had from each exposure; but the second photo used a process which had a negative and positive form. The grainy texture of the original calotype comes from the fact that the negative was made of paper, which meant that any imperfections on the paper negative came through on to the positive.

The buildings involved in the demolition were houses and shops, one of which belonged to the barber, Richard Hawkins, who lived and died in this house.

The view from the Church Tower showed how little change there was after the central houses had gone. What is now Shilcocks was built on the site of *The Six Bells*, pulled down in 1868, but otherwise the changes are largely in the names.

The Corn Exchange, which caused the major change, was opened for business on 22 March, 1853 with 36 stalls and merchant's office. The building belonged to the Market Company who leased the stalls, and the Exchange itself could be hired as an Auction Room or for public purposes as different as promenade concerts, bazaars or political meetings.

Burtons acquired and rebuilt the shop on its right, and next door was *The Swan Hotel*, from which John

Kershaw's coach would set off on his journey to Smithfield, at a charge of 8s. for outside passengers and 16s. for those inside. *The Swan* was sold to Gatwards in 1884 and disappeared in the Arcade of 1927.

Across the road on the corner was the draper's shop which became Brookes, then Jackson's. It was knocked down about 1920 to be rebuilt as a bank.

30 View from St Mary's Church Tower, *c.*1903

31 Market Place looking towards what is now the Arcade, *c.*1875 *Latchmore*

32 Bull Corner (The Triangle) and the entrance to Queen Street

One of the first houses that we know anything about on the Triangle was Isaac Brown's Quaker Academy, opened on premises that had formerly belonged to Thomas Williams, a wool comber. William Lucas recorded in his diary for 10 November 1831: 'Had the whole of Isaac Brown's school to tea—with a young assistant—31.' Some of those boys were later to make a mark in life, not least Joseph Lister, raised to the peerage for his services to surgery, and his brother Arthur who became a famous mycologist. Birket Foster the artist was also educated here, as were William Ransom and many scions of the Quaker families in Hitchin.

The end of this establishment came in 1845 when a great fire destroyed the school room, dining room and back buildings as well as much of the nearby property, in spite of the presence of the fire brigade for whose new hose Brown had subscribed £1 in 1836. The boys escaped in their nightshirts to friendly houses nearby, and the school did not re-assemble in Hitchin.

After the fire, the area was rebuilt and the result can be seen in one of these photographs. On the right is the old *Triangle Temperance Hotel*, which was the headquarters of the North London Cycling Club who met there at weekends on all manner of wheeled transport from tandems to tricycles. Next was the building we now know as *The Lister House Hotel*, and on the other side was *The Half Moon*, for many years a Lucas pub which at one time was kept by George Buller, an expert bee keeper, and on Tuesdays the yard behind the pub would be filled with market visitors' horses.

On the Bridge Street side of the Triangle were the old jettied houses which have now gone to make way for the garage, while the houses one can see in Queen Street were replaced by flats. The house on the corner of Queen Street and Bridge

33 Bull Corner (The Triangle) and the top of Queen Street, 1885   *Latchmore*

34 Jelly's Workshop and the site of the new Town Hall, before 1900 *Latchmore*

35 Brand Street and the Methodist Chapel, *c.*1880

Street was for many years the home of William Woods Goldsmith, described in the 1902 Trades Directory as a veterinary surgeon, inspector under Contagious Diseases (Animals) Act'. Ironically, the road leading away from his house was at one time so unhealthy for man and beast that it was known as Dead Street until Queen Victoria's reign.

A great deal has happened to Brand Street since these two views were taken. The workshop on the corner belonged to the Baptist W.H. Jelly, the tinplate worker. In 1901 this became the site of the new Town Hall which was built in response to a need for better facilities for stage plays and the like. It was built by Geoffrey Lucas and E.W. Mountford at a Cost of £7,300 and was severely criticised by a councillor then, as there was no room to enlarge the building in the future.

Further down on that side of the road was the Methodist Chapel, built in 1834 and enlarged in 1870. On its right, in this view, is a space which was filled in 1903 by the new post office, whose wall beside the chapel was tiled with white glazed facing bricks to shed light into the building. All this and *The Dog* pub have gone in favour of Sainsbury's supermarket.

36 Eviction in Barnard's Yard, 1904 *H.G. Moulden*

Queen Street District

The Queen Street area has always been notable for its strong sense of community spirit, and this is apparent in the picture of the eviction at Barnard's Yard in 1904. Two policemen with Supt. Reynolds are present to deal with possible trouble, but the crowd gazing into Mr. Moulden's camera seems resigned, despite the militant pose of some, such as the man with the wooden leg. The victims of the eviction, Mr. and Mrs. Runner, stand in the centre of their friends, surrounded by all their worldly possessions, and as there were no cottages in Hitchin untenanted at that time, the couple found shelter with other householders in the neighbourhood.

Such excitements were not a regular occurrence, and life in the yards must have been an uphill struggle fought in unsavoury conditions. The report by the London health inspector, William Ranger, spoke in 1849 of the health hazard here, with people living too close together with inadequate facilities, giving rise to conditions that gave part of the street its deserved name of Dead Street.

37 The entrance to Chapman's Yard *Lewes?*

23

38   Queen Street looking north, *c.1890*   *Latchmore*

As a result of Ranger's report, the Hitchin Local Board of Health was set up, and soon had to deal with complaints, such as one from an inspector who on 23 May 1853, reported nuisances at 12 different premises in Hollow Lane and Back Street, including overflowing privies, open dung pits and defective drains. Gradually, steps were taken to counteract this, and by 1854 the town had a new water supply and sewerage system, which led to improved and cleaner housing, and a fall in the death rate and amount of sickness. In honour of the reigning monarch, Dead Street's pessimistic name

was changed to Queen Street, and improvements soon spread. George Beaver noted in his journal for 25 February 1868: 'Called to a fire in Queen Street in some back premises of houses facing Mr. Warren's stone mason's yard, and near to Joyner's timber yard—not much harm done thanks to our water works supply.'

These moves could not solve all problems, and in 1921 Hitchin Urban District Council was to declare Queen Street and some other areas to be insanitary, which led to the demolition of much of the area in the late 1920s.

39   Queen Street looking south, *c.*1886   *Latchmore*

A further period of development altered Queen Street's appearance again in 1956, with the plan to pull down the houses from *The Half Moon* pub to the Congregational Church, and replace them with more modern living accommodation. Thus many of the buildings in these two views of the street are no longer there, though *The Half Moon*, now *The Found Inn*, still stands. In the 1890s it was kept by George Buller, who later became collector of market tolls for the UDC; in his time, market day crowded the inn yard with ponies. Further down can be seen the entrance to Davis Alley and beyond that was the painter and plumber Daniel Grant. He used to store odd lengths of galvanised piping in his yard and would chase the children from the British School (which still stands), when they blew down the pipes to make strange noises.

On the other side of the street, beside Mr. Waller's tent hire yard, were the premises of Edwin Henry Tooley, described in the 1894 Trades Directory as 'corn merchant & miller & manufacturer of the celebrated lambs' food'.

40   One of the small yards off Queen Street   *Lewes?*

41 The family baker, 102-3 Queen Street, *c.*1900 *Latchmore*

42 The possible Tanner's Hall, Queen Street, 1926 *Walter Whiting*

In 1889 George Jackson sold off the property of the late Mr. Daniel Cannon, of which Lot 5 'a dwelling house with baker's shop and premises in Queen Street, in the occupation of Mr. George Garratt, was purchased by the tenant for £270'. By the late 1890s Ernest Crawley was the baker.

At the same time, householders aimed to be self-sufficient, as is shown by the equipment lining the walls of one of the smaller yards. Most of these yards vanished in the demolition of 1925-9 when 174 cottages were removed, which involved the rehousing of 637 inhabitants. Many went fairly happily to the Sunnyside Estate, built largely for this purpose, and so they were able to choose their new home to some extent. Others were less happy and stayed on in their old homes until the last possible minute. The UDC held twice-weekly evening meetings to hear complaints, most of which involved dissatisfaction with receiving the site value and not the true value of their homes as compensation.

The demolitions of 1925-9 were successful in locating many interesting architectural features previously hidden by later additions. The best example of this was a building with an arch-braced frame of oak with early 15th-century mouldings and traces of red paint in places. The wooden framework must once have spanned and supported the open-timbered roof of a town house, and as tradition had located the Hall of the Hitchin Tanners in Queen Street, Hine suggested it might have been this same building.

Barnard's Yard too was interesting, as seven of its houses were much older than their neighbours. Two half-crowns of Elizabeth I's reign were found under a bedroom floor there, and the building materials were mainly of the same date. Cllr. Charles Worbey, whose father appeared in the eviction photo, had strong links with the Queen Street area, and built himself a house at the top of Kershaw's Hill, using Elizabethan bricks, roofing tiles and door steps from Barnard's Yard. Some of the remaining Elizabethan material went to the U.S.A. for use in a replica of Hampton Court.

43 (left) Interior of the possible Tanners' Hall, 1926 *Latchmore*

44 (above) The corner of Queen Street and Portmill Lane, *c*.1900 *Latchmore*

45 (below) Arch from the first floor of the possible Tanner's Hall, 1926

Few pictures in the book can be so unrecognisable as this view northwards along Queen Street. Not one building in this photograph still stands today: all were razed in the radical clearance which began in 1930. The scene runs from Biggin Lane on the far left, right up to Hermitage Road. The Queen Street area had 13 pubs to cater for the needs of its depressed inhabitants, and at least five of these can be located on this view of the street. The only real survivor here is the name of *The Bricklayers Arms*. It is still under the same brewery, but the house was altered in 1922. On the left we now have St Mary's Square and opposite stand the telephone exchange, flats, a new pub and a garage. The pubs now gone include *The Black Lion*, *Two Brewers*, *White Horse* and *Peahen*, the latter brewing its own beer which was sold for 2d. inside the pub, but 1½d. if you drank it outside.

In view of the great changes that have taken place in the Queen Street area since the 1920s, it is difficult to imagine a time when people living in the rest of Hitchin were wary about going near Queen Street. Children were warned to keep away for fear of smallpox or worse, and policemen took care to enter the area in pairs. Before Victorian sanitary improvements affected the area, it was undoubtedly far from healthy and an early history of the town claimed that all the inhabitants of Dead Street perished in the Great Plague of 1665. Later epidemics also left their mark on the area, and even today an excavation in this part of the town sometimes hits an old burial pit of victims of the 18th-century smallpox outbreak or other diseases.

Occupations of the Queen Street folk varied widely, but many were casual labourers, often working for Ransom's, collecting dandelions and other plants. In 1915 people could earn up to £15 a week by doing this, and it was a common sight to see sacks of dandelions emptied into the gully in the middle of each yard to be washed.

46   Queen Street from the entrance to Biggin Lane, *c.*1900   *Latchmore*

47 Thorp's Yard, Queen Street, demolished in 1925 *Lewes*

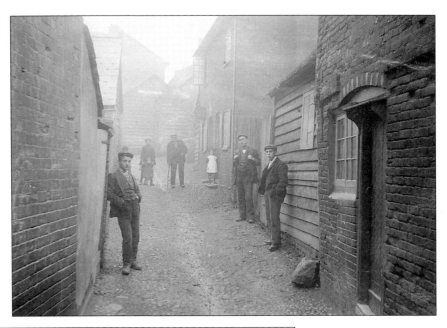

48 Chapman's Yard, Queen Street *Lewes?*

Many of the women did straw plaiting, and in 1874 C.A. Bartlett erected a brick-built Plait Hall near Thorp's Yard for the sale of plait, but the venture failed and in 1898 the Hall was sold to become St Andrew's Church.

Photographs tend to give a slightly distorted impression of a place, as with Chapman's Yard which here looks exclusively residential, but which on the other side was made up of barns. Yard life was earthy, with butchers killing pigs, or people throwing their slops out of their front doors and letting them drain down the centre of the yard.

People knew each other well, partly because of their communal life—for instance, on Sundays the baker in Back Street, Fred Barnett, would light his oven, and people would go along to bake their potatoes there for 1d. Sometimes, men stood on the corner and the children would give them a potato to pass, but there was no real animosity. People now look back on the old Queen Street days with affection, and these photographs remind us of what the area was like before one of the largest schemes of demolition in peacetime removed nearly all trace of the original buildings.

49 Ladies gathered round the pump in the Biggin courtyard *Pearson T. Harris*

Houses

The Biggin and the Hermitage both appear in the later part of this section, but this view of the Hermitage garden recalls several facets of its history. In the early 1800s, when William Wilshere lived there, each summer he would send a basket of strawberries and cauliflowers to Dr. Niblock at the Free School, to exemplify that judicious mixture of utility and luxury which he, as a trustee, felt should be maintained in the curriculum. A later owner, Frederic Seebohm, gave up part of this garden to the town for the creation of Hermitage Road in 1874, but five years later, the garden was still large enough for visitors to comment on the remarkable box hedge which was 50 yards long and 50 feet high.

The other benefactor in the Hermitage Road scheme was another Quaker, the banker James Hack Tuke, who bought the Croft across the road in 1859. This too had a famous garden, with magnolia at the front of the house, a hot house with exotic ferns, a walled garden, a profusion of flowers and shrubs and a little chapel which was later used as a tool shed. Another attraction was a ghost of a grey lady who haunted the chamber over the entrance porch, and caused at least one family of owners to move away, in the early years of our prosaic century.

The house itself originated in the early 15th century and it has been suggested that it was the Woolstaplers' Hall, particularly as shields with the arms of the woolstaplers were found in the Croft during 19th-century renovations. The early plastered timber building was altered in the 17th century and again in the 19th century, when much of what appears on these photographs would have been added. Inside there were fireplaces of blue and white Dutch tiles, and oak panelled rooms, one in the library bearing the initials 'WKB' and the date '1600'. The Croft was demolished in 1964/5 and replaced by a group of four shops whose façade aims to recreate the spirit of the old building.

50 Garden view of the Hermitage, c.1870 *Latchmore*

51 Front view of the Croft, *c.*1866 *Latchmore*[*]

52 Garden view of the Croft, *c.*1866 *Latchmore*

53   The outside of the hall-house, Bancroft

54   The Infirmary, Bedford Road, in the snow   *Latchmore*

Opposite the Croft stood a group of shops at 111-16 Bancroft which were found to include a medieval hallhouse, with gables added in the late 17th century. The house dates from about 1450 and may have been the home of a rich wool merchant, but it had changed status frequently since then. By 1958, when it was demolished, it was used for shops, and the builders of the new Co-operative store tried to make it fit in with the general character of Bancroft.

The hall-house would have been a familiar sight to the lad standing outside the Infirmary, the solid building dating from 1840 on Bedford Road. This makes it slightly later than the Cottage in Wratten Lane to which Thomas Barton Beck retired about 1821. The building had been a farmhouse and had several additions while it was the home of the Becks and the Lucases. For 95 years it was the home of the local artist Alice Mary Lucas who died in 1939 in the bed in which she was born. The house was eventually converted into flats.

The Biggin has seen a great number of uses since its construction in 1361 by Sir Edward de Kendale as a Priory for three Gilbertine canons. Some of the original timbering probably survives in the roof where there are two crown posts and traces of two more, showing that the Priory was built round the central courtyard in which the old ladies were gathered in the earlier photo.

The Priory was dissolved in 1538 and was left empty until 1545 when John Cocks bought for the sum of £254 12s. 9d. the 'whole house and site of the late Priory of the Byggyng and all houses, buildings, yards, orchards, gardens, pools, fish-ponds, land and soil within the site'. Within 25 years it had passed to the Croocar family, and one room carries the initials 'W.C. & I.C. 1585' from their occupation. Soon after this, Robert Snagge, the second son of the owner of Letchworth Hall, made the Biggin his residence and had an extensive re-building programme, into the form which survives today.

56 A staircase in the Biggin

55 The Cottage, Wratten Lane *Latchmore*

57 A room in the Biggin

58   The Almshouse at Starlings Bridge, *c.*1870   *Latchmore*

By 1635 Joseph Kempe had acquired the Biggin and he ran a school there to which pupils came from all over England. His son John continued the teaching, though Joseph's will in 1654 also provided for the care of 'Kempe's Widows'. 1723 saw the Biggin hired by the overseers as an additional workhouse or poor house for the parish, as the Tilehouse Street building was overflowing. In 1812 the overseers bought the Manor House in Bancroft for this purpose, which left the Biggin free to return to the use which Kempe had intended, and since then it has served for almshouses in which each old lady has her own room. In 1890, when the new Hitchin Grammar School was being built, the pillars from the courtyard here formed the model for the school's gallery.

Charities played an important part in the life of a community in the days before the welfare state, and almshouses are a survival of this philanthropy. *An Account of the Hitchin Charities* in 1836 records: 'James Carter, by his will dated in 1660, gave for the use of the poor of the parish of Hitchin, the rents of two tenements in Hounsditch,

London, for the term of a lease which has long since expired. With these rents a house and about a rood of land were purchased at Starlings Bridge, in this parish, which is now occupied by two poor families, who are nominated by the churchwardens. This tenement has lately been put into repair from the produce of some timber which

59   The Tuscan colonnade in the Biggin courtyard

was felled upon the property.' About sixty years later, the almshouses had been sold by the Charity Commissioners, and the £200 proceeds were invested to help other charities.

The final view brings us back to the Hermitage. This building began as a large barn, probably of the 16th century, which was converted into part of a dwelling house in the 18th century, the rest of the house being rebuilt or added at the same time. John Ransom had his flour and corn mill in the large front room, and on his death his daughter Mary Exton lived there, to be followed by her daughter Mary Ann who married Seebohm. The Hermitage estate was bought up in 1927-9 for the building of 29 shops.

60 The Hermitage from Bancroft *Latchmore*

61 Bancroft sheep and cattle market in front of the Hermitage, after 1875 *Latchmore*

Markets

There is no precise information on the date when Hitchin Market first appeared, but there is a document in the Public Record Office which lists the property of John de Baliol who died in 1268, and Hitchin Market is there listed as worth 10 marks. At this stage it would have been a collection of movable stalls catering for the buying and selling of perishable goods and those from elsewhere. Gradually, the stalls gave way to fixed stalls, and then to small shops in the area between Bucklersbury and Sun Street, while at the other end of the selling area, Bancroft retained its great width, suitable for a street market. For at least five hundred years, the history of Hitchin Market was tied up with that of the Lords of Hitchin Manor, and it is when their property was assessed that we find some clue as to how well the market was doing—in 1527 the bailiff took 51s. 4d. in tolls from Hitchin Market, but by 1650 the profits were up to £19. These amounts gained from market tolls fluctuate quite widely over the years, and records show too that attempts were made to keep the area clean—in the early 18th century, for instance, the bailiff was ordered not to make a dunghill in the market, and the market place was to be swabbed down every Tuesday night.

By 1794, the *Universal British Directory* described the town's trade in the following way:

It was formerly famous for the staple commodities of the kingdom, and divers merchants of the staple of Calais resided here, since which that trade is lost; yet the market, which is held on Tuesday (by prescription free from the payment of toll for any sort of corn or grain), has long been, and still is, accounted one of the first in the county for corn, but more particularly so for the quantity and quality of its wheat. The town has no manufactory, but the inhabitants make a great deal of malt. The fairs are kept on Easter Tuesday and Whit Tuesday, for a few cattle, sheep, and pedlary ware.

62 Bancroft sheep market, 1891 *Latchmore*

39

64 Bancroft sheep market, *c.*1895   *Latchmore*

63   Bancroft sheep market with Joe Kingsley, a farmer from Pirton, *c.*1890

65   Bancroft cattle market outside Ransom's

By the middle of the 19th century, Bancroft's market was the source of some agitation, and in George Beaver's Diary for 15 May 1857, he notes: 'Mr. Tuke gives me orders to get him a plan showing all the land between West Lane and Old Park Road—in anticipation of proposal of removal of cattle market "out" of town.' He was asked to plan this area again in 1873 and 1883, the latter after the Local Board received a letter from local farmers and dealers complaining of 'the inconvenience and want of proper accommodation in the sheep and cattle market as at present held in Bancroft. The number of sheep sent to Hitchin on Tuesdays has been on the increase for some years, but the space for penning and showing them to buyers has been much decreased and interfered with by the opening of the new road to the station', namely Hermitage Road.

This plan was abandoned, largely because of the expense, but in 1903 more stringent rules forced the closure of the Bancroft street market, and the cattle and sheep market moved up to a new site by Nun's Close, on land leased for 99 years from

Trinity College, Cambridge. There it has remained, in gradual decline through the 1970s until the site was purchased for redevelopment as a superstore in 1987.

The two views of Hitchin Market Place in the 1890s serve as a reminder of just how important it was as a focal point for the community, no matter whether they were buying, selling or just passing through. The variety of goods available can be seen, as can the one-horse bus owned by Edwin Logsdon at *The Sun* which was for years the chief link between the town centre and the station, at 6d. a time. The market was never dull and people remember all kinds of activity, ranging from dogfights or a runaway horse and cart, to James Rennie the colporteur with his books on his travelling van, or the blind man with his Braille Bible and his dog.

The market made a great difference to trade at Hitchin's pubs, and on Tuesdays *The Sun* had so many carts at the backs that there had to be special reserved spaces. *The Sun* served a special dinner for market days, as did other inns in the town, such as

66 Market Place looking towards Sun Street, 1893 *Latchmore*

67 Market Place looking towards the Corn Exchange, 1895 *Latchmore*

The Swan. This hotel served its Market Ordinary, a sumptuous meal at a moderate cost, and the farmers who attended this meal would wash it down with plenty of ale, so it was not uncommon for people to return home 'market merry'. *The Swan* was sold to John Gatward in 1884 and did not revert to being a hotel.

All the main events in the town's life were held in the Market Place, as can be seen in the section on celebrations. In the late 19th century, the Salvation Army would play in the Market Place every Sunday afternoon, and on 5 November a giant bonfire would be lit in the centre of the square.

By the time that these photographs were taken, the Market Place had lost some of the buildings which had once adorned it. The Shambles which were removed after the Corn Exchange was built can be seen elsewhere in the book, but until 1829 there had been a Bell-House, a Manor-Court House and a Middle Row, all of which were removed as they were impeding the traffic. Soon after, the Market tolls which had formerly belonged to the Crown were obtained by the Market Company, but their lease expired at Michaelmas in 1882, when the tolls were bought by the Local Board for £4,000. This change did not affect the market.

68   Sheep market at Moss's Corner

69   Plait market *c.*1900   *Latchmore*

Any market where livestock is sold is liable to have its problems, and Hitchin is no exception. Possibly the most serious threat came in 1865-6 with the Cattle Plague. In the autumn of 1865, local J.P.s issued an authority to fine anyone £20 who brought any form of cattle to Hitchin Market but this did not stop the spread. St Mary's Church therefore announced: 'In consequence of the continuance of the Cattle Plague, the Clergy of Hitchin (at the desire of the Bishop of the Diocese) request their people to make Friday, March 9th, 1866, A DAY OF SPECIAL PRAYER AND HUMILIATION, for the removal of this calamity.'

By this time George Jackson, the auctioneer, was firmly established in Hitchin, having held his first sale in the town on 27 March 1846. His early sales dealt with 'five entire horses' or 13 Alderney and Guernsey cows, and they soon became weekly sales. In 1878 he bought *The Cock Inn*, soon selling the hotel premises to a local brewing firm, and in

the yard he set up cattle sales and a new site yard office. From his office in Bancroft he held weekly sales of stock, and it was partly to be near his cattle sales that the council moved the market in 1903.

Lighter moments still occurred, and the *Herts. Express* in October 1918 told the tale of a cow which escaped from Jackson's yard, passed under *The Cock Hotel's* archway and bolted upstairs in a jeweller's shop in High Street. Its pursuers caught it there, but they then had to remove a glass swing door in order to return the beast to more appropriate surroundings.

Perhaps the most important aspect of Hitchin Market in the 19th century was its plait market. Arthur Young in his *General View of the Agriculture of Hertfordshire* published in 1813 said: 'There is so much plaiting at Hitchin, that they will not go to service; boys are here also employed in it.'

Generally speaking, people made up their scores of straw plait at home, or in the case of children, at plait schools, and this would then be taken to Hitchin Market. In the 1830s and 1840s they could earn on average 5s. to 7s. a week, though one girl claimed to have received 16s. 2d. for a week's work at the market. In 1874 the Plait Hall was opened on Queen Street which to some extent superseded the market, but trade continued on the market for a long while after that date. The plaiters would gather in the section of the market set aside for them, the corner to the left of the Corn Exchange, and there they would sell their bundles to the men from the Luton factories for about 2d. a score, and then buy bundles of new straw.

Nowadays, the market has moved away from its old setting in the street and Market Place as shown in these photographs. In 1939 when war was imminent, the market was moved to St Mary's Square to provide accommodation for static water tanks in its place in case of incendiary bombs. On its new site there was more room to expand, and the market rivalled that of nearby towns, eventually becoming one of the largest markets in the Home Counties. In 1963 the Market began in West Alley, and six years later plans were drawn up again for a new market site beside the church. St Andrew's School opened on a new site, and over the next few years the area was cleared and the new market was set up. A tablet on the wall nearby records: 'The opening of this market precinct in November 1973 as part of a Town Centre Redevelopment Scheme was undertaken on the joint initiative of the Hitchin Urban District Council and Star (Great Britain) Holdings Limited. This began a new era in the long history of the open-air market in Hitchin which has been a traditional feature of the life of the town since early medieval times.'

70 High Street looking towards Bancroft, on Market day, *c.*1895 *Latchmore*

71 Plait market in the 1880s *Latchmore**

72 Market Place before 1880 *Latchmore**

Inns

The first person to record her opinion of Hitchin ale was Elizabeth I who told the Spanish ambassador who was boasting of his country's vineyards that 'My Hitchin grapes surpass them or those of any other country'. In times before tea and coffee, the Queen drank Hitchin beer at breakfast, but the beer was not always to meet with approval. An anonymous pamphleteer in 1834 said that people mocked 'pale-faced Hitchineers' because of the quality of their beer and said: 'They may well call us pale/for the beer we inhale/is scarce better than that which we call Adam's ale'.

Whatever the quality, and there were plenty of local brews to choose from, Hitchin was well supplied with pubs. In 1849 William Ranger came up from London to report on the health and state of the poor, and he noted that the town had 59 public houses and beerhouses, at a time when Hitchin's population was about 7,000, over half of these being women.

A representative sample of Hitchin's inns appears in the next few pages, many showing that the landlords could often undertake other work as well. John Webb of *The Cooper's Arms* described himself in the 1880s as 'beer retailer and fly proprietor', and this may have given him sympathy with a company of soldiers whom he saw busily grooming their horses, and brought out two great mugs of ale so that they could drink his health. *The Cooper's Arms* is a fascinating building, with substantial remains from the 15th century, but although its true origins are still vague it does not seem to have become a public house until well into the 19th century.

Right down the road from *The Cooper's Arms*, at the far end of Bridge Street, stands what used to be *The Boot Inn* in the 19th century, but became *The Royal Oak* just before 1900.

73 (left) *The Coopers Arms*, Tilehouse Street, *c.*1885 *Latchmore*

74 (right) *The Royal Oak*, formerly *The Boot* *Latchmore*

75 *The Sun* with Col. Somerset and the Hirondelle, *c.*1880   *Latchmore*

76   *The Sun* and *The Angel*, 1870   *Latchmore*

It is appropriate that *The Sun Hotel* should be shown with a coach outside its door, for the hotel owed its increased prosperity to the coaching trade. The first Hitchin coach, in 1706, may well have belonged to the landlord of *The Sun*, but the major figure in this development was John Shrimpton who set up his coaching business in 1741. This was to run, under his relatives the Kershaws, until the coming of the railway forced them out of business in 1850. In Shrimpton's day the coach started from *The Sun*, but the Kershaws moved this to *The Red Lion* and later to *The Swan*. Meanwhile, William Marshall, a mid-18th-century landlord of *The Sun*, became the town's postmaster, and in 1772, three highwaymen held

up a coach at *The Sun* and carved their initials and the date on bricks by the entrance—the date can still be seen over the archway.

In 1876, the coaching link was revived by a Col. Somerset who started a run between *The Sun* and *The George* at Enfield, in his four-in-hand coach, the Hirondelle. The Colonel always drove the vehicle which became the fashionable way to travel, partly as Lord Salisbury let the coach drive through Hatfield Park. By 1886 the charges were 7s. for a single fare on the 3½ hour trip, 10s. return, and an extra 2s. 6d. for the box seats. Though Col. Somerset was a wealthy man, this venture did not add to his income for years, and eventually succumbed to more rapid progress.

Much of the social and legal life of Hitchin revolved round this corner of Sun Street: the Archdeaconry Courts were held at *The Angel*, and from about 1600 the Michaelmas Court Leet and the Sessions were held at *The Sun*. While *The Angel* landlords maintained an angelic manner, one of *The Sun* landlords was in 1619 accused of 'selling drinks in black pots in a quantity less than a pint for one penny', while another went further and attacked a woman gleaner with a pitchfork so she was 'unable to sustain her children or go about her husband's business'. Because of its parliamentary affiliations in the Civil War, *The Sun* waned in popularity for some time, but by the early 19th century it was again an important meeting place for the Cecil Lodge;

the Hitchin & Baldock Bible Association; and the public showing of the Siamese twins born to Mary Fisher of Gosmore. The building of the Town Hall took away such custom, but by then *The Sun* was in the capable hands of the Hills: Samuel and his son William who died in 1888.

While *The Sun* continues, *The Angel* has gone, finally closing on 27 July 1956. It too had a 19th-century dynasty, the Lowdens, William Dixon Lowden being named on the inn sign here. One of his forebears kept a tame deer at *The Angel* which used to go begging for its food at other people's houses, but this, like the building, is now only a memory and the site is filled by shops and a café.

77 *The Trooper*, later Moss's Corner, 1860 *Latchmore*

The photograph of *The Trooper* shows just how close Hitchin's various pubs were to one another in the heart of the town, as there are three more inn signs in view. Here *The Trooper's* landlord, John Carter, stands proudly outside his pub, which soon afterwards became the headquarters of W.B. Moss's grocery and provision business. In 1899 the building was demolished to make way for a new building for Moss's, but another point of interest about *The Trooper* is that it is described variously in Trades Directories as being in Sheep Market, Cattle Market, Church Passage and eventually High Street, showing how long it took for street names to be standardised.

Just down the road stood *The Three Horseshoes* and the inn sign shows the horseshoes facing downwards, as in the badge of the Worshipful Company of Farriers. Anyone else using horseshoes for luck had to hang them facing upwards, but a smith was thought to be too powerful for this to apply to him. The landlord mentioned on the sign, William Woods, was there for the last 20 years of the 19th century, but though the pub continued for over fifty years, the building is now occupied by an estate agent. *The Three Horseshoes* existed before 1800, but *The White Horse* next door had a shorter life, starting in the mid-19th century and ending in the early 1900s, being replaced by the British and Argentine Meat Co., a newsagent and a bank.

Across the street stood *The Cock*, once so well-known for its cock fights that it gave its name to the street. Vestry meetings were held here, and wool, grain and malt brought here for market in the 18th century. Later, *The Cock's* landlord, John Evered, was licensed to let horses and gigs, and one of his horses was stolen in 1818, 'the great gate being lifted off'. Another landlord, John Evans, spent a whole night playing cribbage with some friends from the bank, pausing only to lock the inn at 4 a.m., as the law before 1868 said that an inn must shut for half an hour each day, at the landlord's convenience.

Another of *The Cock's* famous landlords was Alfred Doughty, Vice-Chairman of Hitchin UDC and proprietor of *The Cock* for 28 years. His obituary states: 'He purchased the premises when they were nothing more than a small, old country inn, and enlarged and improved them, until today (1916) *The Cock Hotel* is one of the finest houses in the country.'

The Cock still survives, though it has shifted further down High Street. *The Plough* is no longer a pub, but in 1904 it was advertising the Wild West Show, brought to Hitchin by Buffalo Bill, and the Red Indians of his party caused a mild sensation by setting up their wigwams on the lone prairies of Butts Close.

78 (left) *The Three Horseshoes*, High Street, *c*.1890   *Latchmore*

79 (top) *The Cock Hotel*, High Street, *c*.1880

80 (bottom) *The Plough*, Bridge Street, 1904   *Latchmore*

81 The Woodlands School, now 21 Bancroft, with Joseph Sharples standing in his doorway, 1866 *Latchmore*

Schools

Joseph Sharples, the eminent Quaker banker, died in 1871 and two years later his splendid house on Bancroft became the home of a private select boarding school, the Woodlands, opened by Messrs. Joseph Drewett and Cranston Woodhead. It began with three Hitchin boys out of a total of 21 from all over the country, and the school continued to take boys from the town in its time here. Though originally intended for Quaker boys, this rule was not strictly enforced.

Cycling became popular at the Woodlands early on when, one afternoon, Arthur Latchmore brought his spider-wheel bicycle into the playground. It aroused such enthusiasm that the boys obtained a boneshaker and learned to ride along the Bedford Road. Later a school track was built, which was used while the boys were at lessons by four cycle-mad Cambridge undergraduates who were being coached in Hitchin by Canon Hensley. In 1876, the first Oxford and Cambridge Bicycle Race was held from Hatfield to Cambridge, and Mr. Woodhead allowed the boys to go and watch. Arthur Latchmore had to administer milk to the riders through rubber tubes which he did by joining in at the rider's side on his 46in. bicycle. Much to the glee of the Woodlands boys, the race was won by the Hon. Ian Keith-Falconer, who had been one of Canon Hensley's pupils, and he accomplished this feat in a time of 3 hours 9 minutes on his 60in. bicycle. The photograph taken in 1876 shows what an effect this had at the Woodlands, and even Mr. Woodhead can be seen on the far left with his own penny-farthing bicycle. The cycling craze continued at the school until about 1879 when it began to fade from favour, as bicycling took up time which it was considered should have been devoted to more serious pursuits like cricket or football, which they played against other teams.

82   Bicycle riders at the Woodlands School, 1876   *Latchmore*

83   Caldicott School, Highbury Road   *Latchmore*

Caldicott School was founded at this building on Highbury Road in 1904 by J.H.S. MacArthur and by the man who became its first headmaster, James Heald Jenkins, whose name is commemorated in Jenkins House at the present school. It was a preparatory school for the Leys in Cambridge, though it always had a few boys going to other public schools as well. In the early days, the head had a staff of two resident graduates and a matron, who was a trained nurse. The Hitchin guide for 1909 says that the school 'though distinctly Nonconformist in tone arranges for boys of Church of England parents to attend their own place of worship'. By 1936 the school was planning to move to more extensive premises and in 1938 such premises were found near Slough at Farnham Royal in Buckinghamshire. The school has occupied this site ever since, and it now accommodates 200 boys, as against the 30 of the early days.

At the other side of town, until fairly recent times there stood the Old Free School building which survived 310 years before being demolished in the autumn of 1949 for road widening. The Free School was founded by John Mattock on 25 July 1639, to be financed from the rents and profits of two pieces of land nine acres in total. Various friends gathered

84   The Free School, Tilehouse Street

themselves together to enable Mattock to acquire and rebuild an ancient house on the top of Tilehouse Street 'which time beyond the memory of man had been used for a schoolehouse for the education of the children of the inhabitants of Hitchin'. J.P. Young in his notes on 1949 observed: 'The structure is substantial, but some say not well built. The walls are three bricks thick, laid parallel to each other', but despite any possible deficiencies in the building, it survived many generations of rough use from the schoolboys who worked inside this formidable exterior.

The exact nature of the curriculum to be taught formed the subject of much dispute between the master in charge of the boys and the Trustees in charge of the master. Mattock's will left no precise instructions as to what the children were to learn,

85   W.J. Fitch and members of staff of the Boys' British School, Queen Street

86 The Free School from Paynes Park

thus leaving much room for argument on whether the boys should be given a classical education or just enough training to enable them to cope with a tradesman's life after leaving school. At least one headmaster felt that sons of tradesmen needed no more than 'reading, writing and casting' but in the early 19th century the school came under someone who had different ideas. This was the Rev. Joseph White Niblock who came to the school in 1819 and he was a man of decided views who had printed an English Latin Dictionary and a Greek Grammar, which was used for years at Eton. Unfortunately the Trustees in 1828 adapted the curriculum to the needs of business life with Latin and Greek taught only as extras if required. After enduring this for two years, Niblock left, and following three further masters, his place was taken by John Sugars, one of Niblock's former pupils. He stayed until 1876 but when his health broke down in that year, the Trustees closed the school, and Sugars retired on a small pension to live in a cottage at Mount Pleasant until his death in 1882.

After the doors closed on the Free School, to re-open on a different site 13 years later, the building remained but under different uses. When Mr. W.O. Times bought it, he conducted his Adult Men's classes there for years, and he was happy to show interested people traces of its former glory, in particular a large room which still retained some Jacobean work. When it went, the space was used for a garden to commemorate Reginald Hine.

There is no space here to mention all Hitchin's other schools, but the British School on Queen Street is recalled here in the photograph of its most popular headmaster, W.J. Fitch, and his staff. Trained at Borough Road, Fitch came to the Boys' British School as head in 1854 and left in 1899, three years before he died. He admitted exactly 3,333 boys to the school in his time, plus the 160 there when he arrived and was a well-known Hitchin figure. J.R. Curry, when writing his memories of the Hitchin of his youth, saw the grave of Fitch and 'I instinctively stopped and bared my head. I recall his fine presence, his snow-white hair, the extreme neatness of his dress, the quiet humour and dignity of him. It means much that, as a boy, I wished for more when he read the Bible. His lesson on language I remember to this day.' Though a believer in stern discipline, Fitch was well-liked and for years after his death, the school was known as Fitch's.

87 The garden of the Free School *Latchmore*

88   The garden of the Woodlands   *Latchmore*

Despite their differences, there were quite a few points of contact between the Woodlands and the Free School, dating from 1632 when the old house on the Woodlands site was sold to Thomas Papworth by John Mattock. After the Free School closed, the Woodlands continued and in 1879 had three cases of scarlet fever who were transferred to the old Free School to recover, one of these boys being E.V. Lucas, the writer. Ten years later, the Woodlands closed and the premises went to the governors of the Free School's successor, the Grammar School, for £3,100. In May 1889 it opened its doors to boys and girls, and although new buildings sprang up nearby, the girls were on this site until 1908 and boys until the 1930s.

The gardens were kept in immaculate order as seen in the photograph, though one gardener was sacked for selling the owners of the Woodlands produce from their own garden. It was used for Natural History study, with one boy made curator of the birds, being responsible for every nest and on occasions helping the headmaster to keep the cat away from the birds at night. In what had been Sharples' Vinery, the boys set up an Aviary, and in the old stables these Woodlands boys kept pets which they obtained through *Exchange & Mart* or from Hitchin Market, while in early days kingfishers could be seen in the grounds.

89   Students at the Ladies' College at Benslow House, June 1872   *Latchmore*

In the 1860s plans were made to set up a Ladies' College, despite the prejudice against the idea of higher education for mere females. Cambridge was considered unsuitable because of the dangers of fraternisation, so Hitchin was eventually chosen as it fulfilled the necessary conditions of rurality, healthiness and accessibility by rail. The *Herts. Express* in 1868 praised the scheme as 'the social distinction would be accompanied by more solid advantages; for lady students have bodies to be fed and clothed as well as minds to be cultivated and the establishment of the college would increase our local trade by annual thousands of pounds.' Seebohm championed the project for

different reasons and suitable accommodation was found in Benslow House. This large building near the station had belonged to John Ransom but he died in 1867 and his son Alfred agreed to let it for the new College. It opened in late 1869 with six students, two of whom were Quakers, under the supervision of Mrs. Manning, authoress of *Ancient India*. Run in connection with Cambridge, the College submitted candidates for the Tripos in 1872, when the lease of Benslow House was extended for another year, but in October 1873 it re-opened in new premises at Girton, just outside Cambridge, and Hitchin lost its unique link with the new style of education.

90 The Quaker graveyard, with the Infirmary in the background *Latchmore*

91 St Mary's Church, with the school playground in the right foreground, 1866 *Latchmore*

Churches

In *A Quaker Journal*, William Lucas reports for 24 January 1841, 'At our Preparative Meeting today, it was reported that all the Bills for the New Meeting House have been sent in and paid. The total cost, including the warming apparatus, has been £2,115 19s., of which £717 was raised by the sale of the Old Meeting House and forms, and the remainder, £1,398 19s. by subscription from Friends.' The old building in West Alley was built in 1694 in the more tolerant times following religious persecution and lasted until the need arose for a bigger home. In 1958 circumstances again necessitated a move, and the exciting new Meeting House was built by Paul Mauger, a Quaker from Welwyn Garden City, over the old graveyard, in such a way that only about twenty graves were disturbed.

92 Canon Lewis Hensley and the newly cast bell at St Mary's church door, 1901

93 Cooper cottages, West Alley—Joshua Whiting, Latchmore's uncle, by the site of Hitchin's first Quaker Meeting House *Latchmore*

The coming of the Great Northern Railway to a site so far from the centre of Hitchin led to a spate of building in this area, not least of this being St Saviour's Church and its linked buildings. Naturally, there were also members of other religious denominations in this region, particularly Baptists, for whom the old Tilehouse Street Church was quite a walk. In 1867 Richard Johnson, Chief Engineer with the GNR, decided to erect a mission hall on a piece of land he had already bought with a view to building a home for himself. The result was the unusual iron chapel that appears in the photograph, and being of an unusual design, it became the subject of a satirical verse which portrayed Mr. Johnson going to a shop in which:

They always keep Ebenezers of cast iron
A Bethel or two (and in this establishment)
One very small—called 'Mission Hall'—
(At a price it was not made for)
Was doubled up soon,
And the same afternoon
Sent off—GNR—carriage paid for.

The local paper was later to say: 'It cannot he denied that the mission room when it was first put up was not ornamental, but it was intended to be, and has been eminently, useful, and that is the best justification for its existence.'

Opening on 7 December 1867, the project was so successful that within two years it was decided to make the mission into a separate church

94   The iron Baptist Chapel, Walsworth Road, 1869   *Latchmore*

from its parent body at Tilehouse Street. By 1875 the congregations were large enough to warrant the building of a larger chapel, namely the present church.

The earlier photograph of St Mary's Church gives a splendid impression of how the building dominates the centre of the town. This is the latest in a sequence of buildings dating back to 792 when Offa of Mercia founded on this site a Benedictine monastery, which was burnt down in 910. A second attempt was likewise ill-fated, with damage by lightning and an earthquake in the 1290s; the roof eventually collapsed in 1304. Undeterred, the town set out to rebuild the church and their efforts can still be seen in some of the

church's fabric, although many changes have taken place since the church re-opened in 1305— additions and improvements vie with periods of neglect and destruction.

Repairs are always needed for some part of a building as old as the church, and in 1901 it was the turn of the bells to be checked and the tenor bell to be altered. Other types of music came from the Church of England Temperance Society's Drum and Fife Band, under the voluntary instruction for many years of G.B. Bailey, here seen in a light topper. Other sects too had their societies, and the Adult Sunday Schools, founded in 1860, were strongly Quaker, and dealt with anything from singing to pure education.

95 The Church of England Temperance Society's Drum and Fife Band, with Mr. G.B. Bailey and the Rev. J.H. Greaves seated, 1889

96 Frederic Seebohm's Hitchin Adult Sunday School Class *Latchmore*

97   The original Queen Street Congregational Church before its demolition in 1869   *Latchmore*

Paternoster's *Advertiser* for May 1856 recorded the changes in the Queen Street Congregational Church in the following way:

The Old Independent Meeting House was the first Conventicle erected in the town, and is known to have been registered for worship as early as 26 April 1690. The new Chapel is built in the Italian style of architecture near the site of the old building and it greatly adds to the improvement of that part of the town.

Thus baldly they outlined a history which began after the Toleration Act of 1690 when the small group of Independents in Hitchin bought part of an orchard on the east side of Dead Street from Widow Bonfield and built their Meeting House. Major repairs were carried out in 1812 and 1844, but in 1853, 'owing to the dilapidation and inconvenience of the old chapel, the congregation resolved to erect a new sanctuary and to convert the old one into a school room'.

The old building which appears in this picture remained in use as a schoolroom until 1869 when it was pulled down to make way for new Schoolrooms built on to the new chapel. This went on for a 100 years, by the end of which this building too was suffering serious maintenance problems, and after long negotiations the members of the church left their historic site and moved to join forces with the Methodists in the new Christchurch.

98 The Wesleyan Methodist Chapel in Brand Street in Brand Street, before the alterations in 1870 *Latchmore*

When George Whitefield stood up in Hitchin's Market Place to preach, some ill-wishers broke into the church belfry and so jangled the bells that he could not be heard, and it was many years before Methodism gained a foothold in the town. In 1828 they applied for a licence to hold their meetings in a house in Tilehouse Street. As it was next to *The Three Tuns*, they moved in 1829 to what is now 107 Bancroft, and the next year saw them move again to old maltings on Brand Street which were purchased for the purpose by leading Methodists. In 1834 it was decided to build a new chapel on this site, and this was opened on 24 July that year.

In 1870 over £1,000 was spent on modifications to the original building, including the front elevation that survived to the end. The other change was in the music for which Methodism is famous—in their early church, the singing was accompanied by a band of fiddles, clarinet, flute, trombone and bass-viol, the latter played by W.B. Moss's father. This was replaced in the 1850s by a harmonium which in turn gave way to an organ in 1878 and a larger organ in 1881. The last change came in 1965 when the Trustees of this Chapel sold the site to Sainsbury's, and on 21 June 1969 the new Christchurch building on Bedford Road opened its doors for worship by Methodists and Congregationalists together.

Mills

Sixteenth-century records mention an Ickleford Mill, but long before this time, water mills played a vital role in community life, when the people had to grind their grain at the mill of their lord or his tenant. The scene here shows the 19th-century buildings which had an overshot wheel, and the mill now uses electric power.

Ickleford also had a Court Leet House, built in 1599 by another miller, Richard Lucas, who had the leases of Hitchin's Crown Mills of Port Mill and Shooting Mill. The latter was gutted by fire and rebuilt in 1814 on a larger scale by John Ransom. This, with its new name of Grove Mill, also saw attempts to set up a silk mill, but this had failed long before a fire in 1889 raged through the building, defying the efforts of the Hitchin Fire Brigade to stop it. After this, it ceased to function as a mill and became a factory and offices.

In 1824 rain so affected the water level at Grove Mill and Purwell Mill that outhouses and stables were partly washed away, but by 1882 a sale catalogue was able to announce that Purwell Mill was 'well placed on the River Pur, first mill on the stream, with a never failing supply of water, and admirably adapted for steam power, if required'. The catalogue describes the Mill as a 'substantially-erected brick and slated water flour mill, the principal walls of which are fourteen inches thick' and also mentions that it was capable of storing 600 loads of corn. It had a wrought and cast-iron overshot wheel, 12 ft. diameter by 6 ft., and a water wheel shaft with counter gear, driving three pairs of stones.

In the early 20th century, Purwell Mill was still running 5½ days a week, closing midday Saturday, and four-wheeled horse-drawn wagons called to make collections, even after the First World War. Ironically, however, in view of the earlier comments, in 1921 a long summer wind dried up the river so that the Mill could not operate, but it survives to this day, modernised and put to different uses.

100   Grove Mill *Latchmore*

99 (left) Ickleford Mill from the back *Latchmore*

101 Purwell Mill and the house

102   River scene at West Mill   *Latchmore*

103   The farm buildings at West Mill   *Latchmore*

104   The cottages by Grove Mill   *Latchmore*

West Mill, built and occupied by Edward Lucas in the early 1600s, was rebuilt in the 18th century, and survived until a fire destroyed all but some brickwork, the race and sluice in 1961. Its best known miller was Samuel Allen, 1771-1868, who became the tenant on the death of James Whittingstall in 1807. Ill-health had forced him to give up his brewery business, but he remained at West Mill for 22 years, with many visits from his wife's family, the Lucases. One relative, William Lucas, remembered one amusement as punting on the River Oughton in an old flat-bottomed boat. He also noted that 'in the severe winter of 1813-14, West Mill was cut off from us for some weeks by the deep snow which quite filled up the road from the top of the hedge on one side to the other'.

The buildings on the right of picture 103 are of the farm purchased in 1912 by the County Council for smallholdings. There were 16 acres of woods and marsh, the shooting and fishing rights, and very good arable land and grass.

Although a river was vital to the running of a mill, it could also serve for amusement, as at Charlton, or annoyance. The latter occurred in the 1850s when the Hiz, here flowing sweetly in front of the Grove Mill cottages, was the cause of a long and acrimonious court case between the miller Joshua Ransom and the Local Board. He had added ovens to Grove Mill and was selling bread in Hitchin, but the efficient working of his mill was, according to his claim, impeded by the fact that the Local Board had reorganised the treatment of sewage so that it was discharged into the Hiz just above his Mill. Ransom claimed that the new sewage works had 'converted the Mill into a great privy, in constant use, and the mill head into a disgusting cesspool from the filth deposited along the bed of which arise millions of bubbles constantly discharging their mephitic gas and giving it the appearance of being in an active state of fermentation'. Eventually his claims were upheld; the Local Board became liable for high damages so they dissolved rather than pay.

105 Skating at Charlton Mill, December 1874 (Samuel Lucas sketched a very similar scene in 1855)

106   Punting at Charlton Mill, 1868   *Latchmore*

Charlton Mill was mentioned in Domesday Book of 1086, and later passed through the hands of the Knights Templar and Hospitaller. In 1670 it was mentioned in a court case concerning its miller Edmund Papworth, and in 1813 when the Crown sold off its mills by auction, Charlton was bought by William Bodger who also bought Port Mill in Hitchin.

Despite its idyllic appearance, Charlton Mill has not been without its share of excitement. William Lucas's Diary for 27 July 1842 records:

A remarkable thunderstorm this evening. E. Burr's windmill at Charlton was struck by lightning. One of the sails was shivered and the fluid appears to have been conducted by the chain of the sack tackle from the top of the mill to the lowest floor with little injury, the chain ending near the floor, though electricity appears to have flown off in all directions, tearing up the floor, dashing all the glass of the windows, breaking through the

brickwork at the bottom of the mill where it is three feet thick and ploughing the ground in several places outside. The links of the chain were welded together but no appearance of fire in any other part of the mill. The flash was extremely vivid so as to almost dazzle my eyes, although our bedroom blinds were down and a lamp burning in the room, the crash of thunder immediately following was terrific, and terrified many persons who jumped up from bed thinking some injury had been sustained close at hand. The rain fell for some time in torrents.

The best known miller was probably Edward Burr, now immortalised in Sainsbury's mural, and he began as a miller for Samuel Allen at West Mill. He later became the tenant of Charlton Mill and a visitor wrote to the local paper remembering:

… there was something extremely fascinating for us youngsters about the old mill, the house and garden and the mill dam, for we knew that a visit to it usually meant a spice of adventure in the crazy old boat which we punted about the quiet weed-choked water at the peril of our lives ... The tall arbor vitae growing by the waterside, where nests abounded, and the ivy-covered and moss-lined summer-house and boat-house were duly searched for the cunning nesting places of the wren, tomtit and robin ... Some years there was a family of cygnets and we well remember the solicitude of the miller that the swans should not be disturbed.

Edward Burr and his sister Mary were part of the Charlton scene for many years. He died aged 77 in 1863, 'a confirmed, and I fear irreclaimable, bachelor' according to Lucas, and Burr's estate was sold by Jackson at *The Sun* on 23 February 1864 to Mr. Delmé Radcliffe for £2,750. By 1887 it had been leased by the Priory to Arthur Lewin but the end came on 7 March that year when the fire brigade minutes record:

The Brigade was very soon on the spot with No.2 engine ... with a plentiful supply of water from the mill head the fire was soon got under but not before the mill was burnt clean out and the greater part of the roof of the house considerably damaged. The Brigade and Engine remained on duty all the next day; Engine returned to the Station on Tuesday night, leaving two firemen on duty. On Sunday, March 13, two firemen were again placed on duty—the grain still smouldering.

George Beaver noted this fire in his diary and said that the house had been rebuilt after the fire but the mill had not.

Of the mill shown in the photographs, only the wheel survives, after the fire of 1887. Its near neighbour, the windmill at Charlton, kept going with the

107 Edward Burr and his sister Mary at Charlton *Latchmore*[*]

grinding of meal until it was blown down in 1894 but the watermill now no longer catered for the needs of those local gleaners who wanted their corn making into flour, and they went instead to West Mill.

108 Charlton Mill from the road *Latchmore*[*]

The Railway

In 1842, Queen Victoria travelled by rail for the first time. This royal approval of the new mode of transport, and the prospects of vast profits for contractors and shareholders alike, led to the two years of 'Railway Mania' between 1844 and 1846. During this time, 815 Railway Bills were put before Parliament. The feasibility of a London-to-York railway was discussed in Hitchin in 1844, and the Great Northern Railway Act was passed two years later.

There was still animosity from some local landowners; Hitchin Station is a long way from the town centre owing to the opposition of Lord Dacre, who, like Wordsworth and Wellington, felt that mobility of the lower classes would damage the fabric of society. Work on the Great Northern Railway began in 1847, however, and on 7 August, 1850, the first public train left London bound for Peterborough. Hitchin had 12 trains to London on weekdays, and four on Sundays, the fastest reaching the city in 44 minutes. The single fare was 5s. 9d. 1st class, 4s. 2d. 2nd class, and 2s. 7d. 3rd class.

In 1857, the Leicester-to-Hitchin line opened, and Midland Railway trains shared the line into London with the Great Northern. This caused many problems—in 1862 alone there were 3,400 delays. The situation was resolved when the Midland opened the direct Bedford-St Pancras line in 1868.

Hitchin Station attained its present form when rebuilt in 1910, after public protest at the lack of facilities and the narrowness of the footbridge, known locally as 'The Hitchin Alps'.

The railway no doubt contributed to the doubling of Hitchin's population between 1850 and 1923, and the bulk of the extra housing was built between the town centre and the station. Local firms benefited from the new markets which became available to them; it is no accident that the later 'Industrial Area' grew at the north-eastern corner of the town.

110 Some of the staff with two of the shunting horses

109 (left) The staff of Hitchin Station, c.1906 *Herbert Minnis*

111 One of Stirling's passenger locomotives, built in 1867

73

74

112 No.53, a six-foot single built by Hawthorn's of Newcastle in 1848

113 Four engines in the Hitchin yard, *c.*1886 *Latchmore*

114 Growler cabs awaiting the next train in the 1870s *Latchmore*

115 After the railway accident at Litlington in 1866, this engine was brought to the Hitchin sheds. It was made by Sharpe, Atlas Works, Manchester, in 1848 *Latchmore*

116 'Arriving at *The Sun Hotel* a halt was made to enable Mr. Latchmore to photograph the engine', 21 April, 1887 *Latchmore*

The Fire Brigade

'For beer to John Samm—pitching the Ingins—3d.' This bill in the Churchwardens Accounts for 1752 indicates the rather casual approach to the maintenance of the fire-fighting equipment in the mid-18th century.

The Churchwardens had begun the history of the Hitchin Fire Brigade around 1720, when they had bought two engines for £21. These engines were very simple, basically a wooden tank on four wheels, with a hand-operated brass pump on the top. The maintenance consisted of coating the interior of the tank with pitch to keep it watertight, or replacing the pump fittings. All payments in respect of fires were in terms of liquid refreshment, for pumping the water was an arduous task, undertaken by teams of men recruited when the need arose. The beer was such an incentive that it was popularly suspected that many a burning hayrick had been

117   The 1871 manual engine outside Paynes Park Fire Station, with Captain Logsdon nearest the camera   *Latchmore*

118   Some of the brigade at the fire at Grove Mill, 16 September 1889

maliciously lit to ensure a plentiful supply of ale.

The fire equipment was stored in St Mary's porch: the engines and their attendant buckets rarely gathered much dust, for in the 18th century the town's buildings were still largely wooden and fires broke out frequently.

Matters became worse in 1783, when there was a serious outbreak of arson, prompted by the attempts at Parliamentary reform. Letters were found threatening Baldock, and in Hitchin between October and February there were 13 serious fires. These outbreaks continued sporadically for some years.

The election of Robert Newton as a Churchwarden in 1814 produced many changes. He transferred the administration of the engines from the Churchwardens to a new Hitchin Fire Establishment, composed of Churchwardens, agents of insurance companies and leading inhabitants of the town. Instead of casual volunteer pumpers, engines were to he manned by a Hitchin Fire Brigade of 24 men in the charge of Robert's son Isaac; instead of the casual 'ingenears', the engines were to be maintained by the Newton family and stored on their business premises in Tilehouse Street. Although this caused domestic problems when a fire broke out on washday and the washing lines had to be cut and horses trampled the Newtons' washing, the new arrangement was a great improvement. The money for maintenance and improvements was obtained partly from public subscriptions and partly from the

119 The 45 horsepower Mercedes tractor outside the Fire Station in 1918 *Latchmore*

insurance companies; a new engine was bought in 1834, and a public meeting in 1836 subscribed £58 4s. for a new hose, the old one having proved defective at a fire in the Market Place. Outgoings still had a familiar sound: Isaac Newton charged £5 for 'expenses incurred on 19 October 1838, for three pairs of post horses, turnpikes, post-boys, refreshments and pay of the Fire Men'. Pumping the engine was still hard work, hence the beer. No horses were kept specifically for fire duties, and the Captain had to hire what he could when the need arose. The Hitchin Brigade did not restrict its attentions to the confines of the town, and the surrounding villages frequently summoned their aid; the brigade attended a fire in Wymondley, and the engine was taken on

a wagon to assist at the disastrous fire at Luton Hoo in 1843, and attended at Ashwell in 1850 when fire made 200 people homeless.

A new manual engine was obtained in 1871, a Shand-Mason which with 22 men on the pump could raise 100 gallons per minute to a height of 120ft. The brigade's minute book remarked 'Proved to be a powerful engine and gave great satisfaction'. It cost £122.

Isaac Chalkley became Superintendant of the Brigade in 1875, a post which he was to hold for 20 years. He attended some eighty-five fires, the first of which destroyed a notable landmark, Mr. Tuke's windmill on Windmill Hill. Chalkley was an extremely efficient and popular man, and made two notable

120　　Isaac Chalkley and the Brigade in 1881—the building behind is the old Fire Station in Great Yard, off the Market Place, beside *The Rose and Crown Latchmore*

innovations. The first was an annual meeting and supper, held on 5 November. Such were the festivities held in the town on that day that their dinner was rarely finished before they were called out.

Chalkley's second innovation was the more important—a steam fire engine. It was a Shand-Mason double-acting vertical engine with an inclined water-tube boiler, and arrived at Hitchin Station on 21 April 1887. The minute book records:

The men … proceeded to the station on the Manual Engine in their full uniform. The Brigade mounted the steamer and then were followed in procession by the Baldock and Shefford Brigades: arriving at *The Sun Hotel* a halt was made to enable Mr. Latchmore to photograph the engine, after which it was taken to the Park … the engine fire was lighted and in 8 min. 55 sec. steam at 100lbs. pressure was raised. The manner in which the engine worked gave complete satisfaction.

It was noted by many how suddenly arson ceased to be a problem, now that men were no longer needed to man the pumps. Fires still occurred, and they were still dangerous: at a fire in Bendish a year later Fireman Barham was standing on a cottage roof when it collapsed, and he with it into the flames below. It transpired that only his dignity had been hurt, for he fell straight into a cesspit beneath; but this was not the only indignity he and the brigade had suffered: at St Ippollitts in 1881 they had been pelted with onions for refusing the villagers' assistance. Onions henceforth became a feature on the menu at the annual supper.

Isaac Chalkley resigned in 1895 on account of his advancing years and was succeeded by Edwin Logsdon. His tenure of office brought the Hitchin Brigade to an excellence unsurpassed by any other country town. He introduced monthly drills and

121 Chalkley and the Brigade at a practice in Priory Park *Latchmore*

monthly inspection of the hydrants. Electric bells were installed in firemen's homes in 1901 to speed their turn-out, and to commemorate the Coronation of Edward VII, a specially designed fire station was built in Paynes Park and opened in 1904; it cost £711.

Better communications and facilities could not always defeat inclement weather, however, in the winter of 1911 the firemen had to cut steps in the ice-covered road up Offley Holes Hill before the fire engine could be pulled up by four horses, with all the men behind pushing.

The horses were replaced in 1917 by a 45-horsepower Mercedes tractor with 1,950 ft. of hose, a far cry from the inventory of a half-century earlier, which listed 'Two large engines (complete), Two small old ditto, 20 lengths of Hose (40 ft.) ... 1 long ladder ... 130 buckets ... 2 iron Fire hooks ... 1 hand engine ... Quantity old hose, etc. etc ...'

Another Shand-Mason vertical steam engine was bought in 1918, but was made redundant in 1924 when the brigade bought a Morris-Guy Petrol Engine with a 150-200 gallon turbine pump. The brigade became a County responsibility in 1948.

122 Edward VII's Coronation celebrations, Market Place, 9 August 1902 *Latchmore*

Celebrations

124 Queen Victoria's Golden Jubilee decorations, Market Place, and High Street corner, June 1887 *Latchmore*

On 24 June 1902, two days before Edward VII's Coronation should have taken place, a telegram came to Hitchin, reading: 'Coronation postponed. King undergoing operation.' Though saddened by the news of their King having to endure this new-fangled appendix operation, his Hitchin subjects decided to scrap their intended pageantry and festivities, but to retain the treats for the children and old people, which took place on 26 June, as previously arranged.

Unlike the food for the treats, the pageantry could be set aside and brought out on the new Coronation date, and therefore on 9 August 1902 the Hitchin Celebration of the King's Coronation emerged as a splendid procession with an accompanying booklet written by Wentworth Huyshe, the author and prominent member of Hitchin's Society of Arts and Letters. This involved 28 sections showing various aspects of life in the town and in the King's

123 (left) Queen Victoria's Golden Jubilee decorations, Market Place, June 1887 *Latchmore*

empire. The Hitchin Fire Brigade took part, and the three floats in the foreground of the photograph display the 'Brig Chorister', 'Nations of the World' and 'Sports'. At the conclusion of the procession, the Royal Standard was hoisted in the Market Place by the Chairman of the District Council, and everyone sang 'God Save the King'.

Later in the afternoon, there was a decorated cycle parade, and in the evening a Grand Carnival Masquerade and Torchlight Procession, and finally fireworks and a bonfire on Butts Close.

In the booklet compiled for the occasion, W.O. Times wrote: 'The Hitchin Permanent Coronation Memorial will take the form of a new Fire Station, towards the cost of erection of which a considerable sum of money has been collected. Any balance of the money subscribed for the festivities will be devoted to this fund.'

It is thus fitting that Captain Logsdon and his team of Hitchin firemen should appear in this view of the day's procession.

125   Queen Victoria's Golden Jubilee decorations, *Sun Hotel*, June 1887   *Latchmore*

It was of course some time since Englishmen had celebrated a coronation because of Queen Victoria's long reign. She came to the throne on 20 June 1837 and 50 years later her Golden Jubilee was celebrated. The day after became a public holiday so George Beaver's Diary notes the events of that 21 June 1887:

All the shops of the town are closed and business ceases at 1p.m.—in the afternoon the Sunday school children of all denominations, with their teachers etc. attend a United Jubilee Service at St Mary's Church at 3p.m. ... On leaving the church they all assemble in the Market Square and from thence adjourn to their several chapels and schools to have tea and pastimes ... In the evening at 7.30 a special Jubilee choral service at St Mary's with address by the Vicar—Church quite full ... After the mid-day service the Rifle Volunteers under Lieutenant F. Preedy ascended the Tower of the Church and from thence fired off a 'feu-de-joie' and some 'volley firing' with very good effect. In the afternoon between three

and four-hundred people of both sexes from 60 years of age and upwards have a comfortable tea-dinner in the Corn Exchange and a public dinner to working people and their wives, of any age, is given to over 2,000 in Bancroft ... In the evening tile town is tastefully and profusely decorated with flags and banners and illuminated by gas and oil, a good display, and a bonfire with fireworks in Butts Close late in the evening.

An idea of how cheerful these flag displays were can be seen in these three views.

Queen Victoria died on 22 January 1901, and the Hitchin Board of Guardians recorded their feelings in a resolution: 'That this Board desire to record their deep and heartfelt sorrow at the loss of their beloved Queen, to express their respectful sympathy with the Royal Family, and to assure his Majesty of their unfaltering loyalty to the Throne.'

A strict schedule was issued for the formal announcement of King Edward's accession, which read: Sir George F. Faudel-Phillips, Bart, GCIE,

126 Edward VII's Proclamation, Market Place, 29 January 1901—The High Sheriff reads the proclamation in the centre, and on the white horse to the right is the Chief Constable of Hertsfordshire, Col. Daniels   *Latchmore**

High Sheriff of the County, is charged with the the Proclamation of his Majesty King Edward the Seventh in Hertfordshire.

The High Sheriff, accompanied by his Under-Sheriff, Mr. C.E. Longmore, will reach Hitchin Railway Station, at 11.38 a.m., on Tuesday, the 29 January 1901 and escorted by a detachment of the Herts. Constabulary, will at once proceed to the Market Place.

He will be met at the Market Place by the Chairman and Members of the Urban District Council, and the County Justices.

He will be received by a Guard of Honour of the 1st VB the Bedfordshire Regiment, at the shoulder. He will proclaim the King, and after a flourish from the Sheriff's Trumpeters, the Guard of Honour will give a Royal Salute.

The High Sheriff will leave Hitchin by the train leaving there at 12.37 p.m.

All flags will be flown at the masthead during the ceremony, and be lowered to half-mast after it is over.

127 Queen Victoria's Diamond Jubilee celebrations, Bancroft, 22 June 1897 *Latchmore*

128 Guests at the opening of the new Water Tower, Windmill Hill, 6 September 1909, with Theodore Ransom in a panama on the far left *Latchmore**

The flags must have had quite a good airing at this period, as in 1897 they had been out again to celebrate Queen Victoria's Diamond Jubilee.

Paternoster and Hales published the official programme of the Hitchin Celebration of this unique event, which began on the Monday of that June week with tea for the Sunday schoolchildren at the Football Field on Bedford Road, and the presentation to them of a jubilee mug and a bun. 'Every effort has been made to secure for the children an outing that shall long be remembered by them and with flags, banners, two bands, and an abundance of provisions they should have a happy day.'

Tuesday followed a similar pattern, with a procession of Hitchin Societies round the town. At 1.30p.m. the old people had dinner at the Corn Exchange with a concert by the Banjo Orchestra and other Hitchin celebrities. Children not in the Sunday schools received their tea, jubilee mugs and bun at the Corn Exchange, and there were more sports at the Football Field. At 9.30 p.m. another parade wound round the town, this time the Grand Carnival Masquerade and Torch-light Procession, and it all finished with fireworks in the Market Place and at Butts Close a bonfire and ascent of fire balloons with magnesium lights.

No such frivolities accompanied the opening of the Water Tower on 6 September 1909. Three years earlier an enquiry had revealed that the 'town is often on the verge of a water famine on account of the inadequacy of the storage tanks'. At a cost

of £11,000 this sorry state of affairs was remedied, and the then Chairman of the UDC, Theodore Ransom, invited guests to the official opening of this new high-level service tower tank on Wind-mill Hill. Lawson Thompson opened the tower and reservoir, then turned on the water and said that he hoped the tower 'will handsomely supply every house in the town with good water for many years to come'.

Hitchin seems to have relished celebrations throughout its history, beginning with its May Day festival, which involved fixing branches of May on the doors of respectable people in the town, and shaming those who had not behaved by putting a branch of elder and nettles outside their house. The Mayers would then dance and frolic through Hitchin, with two men with their faces blackened, one dressed as Mad Moll and the other as her hunchback husband wielding a broom which he would use to attack any of the crowd whom he claimed had abused his wife.

This carried on into the 19th century, and William Lucas's tale of Queen Victoria's coronation celebration is also lively: 'At a meeting summoned on the spur of the moment it was proposed to give a dinner to all the children between the ages of six and fourteen. Accordingly today more than 1,200 children have partaken of good old English fare in Bancroft.' After other feasting, during which the ladies at the Biggin were made to drink the Queen's health in punch, 'an immense concourse assembled in Butts Close at 5 o'clock to witness ludicrous sports such as donkey racing, catching a pig with its tail soaped, hunting the Bell man, etc.'

Celebrations persisted, with Hitchin having flamboyant processions on 5 November each year. The local paper recorded disapprovingly that 'the day has been seized upon for a display of a grotesque mixture of pyrotechnics and masquerading, and having no connection whatever with so-called religious feeling'. By 1882 the paper was able to report: The Carnival demonstration, which for some years has marked the fifth of November in Hitchin, has this year been allowed to die out. On Monday evening, a few people assembled in the Market Place, and a few fireballs were carried about and some fireworks let off, but the heavy rain soon put an end to any display, and by 9 o'clock the town wore its usual quiet appearance.

There is always an excuse for processions, and in 1899 Bank Holiday Monday saw the Cart Horse & Tradesmen's Turn-out Parade. Echoes since include the Hitchin Pageant to celebrate the Festival of Britain, royal occasions and the annual Carnival Parade in aid of local charities.

129   Cart Horse and Tradesmen's Parade, Market Place, 7 August 1899   *Latchmore*

130   Cart Horse and Tradesmen's Parade, with Alfred Saunders, a firewood dealer from Gosmore, in the foreground, 7 August 1899   *Latchmore*

131 Joseph Whiting and his family in their garden at Bancroft

132 William Maylin, the Walsworth centenarian (1803-1905) *Latchmore*

Hitchin Characters

The following photographs give only a brief idea of some of Hitchin's characters, starting with the Whiting family group. Joseph was the fellmonger who resigned as a Quaker and became a Congregationalist on his marriage. He died at the age of 73, a youngster compared with William Maylin (1803-1905). He worked for Messrs. Jeeves for over fifty years as bricklayer and archcutter and his greatest ambition was to ride in a car. W.B. Moss took to attending meets in a car when he became unable to ride, but before he had been a great lover of horses and a keen rider to hounds. William Ransom appears beside his coach elsewhere, but here stands in his Fairfield garden, resting from his busy life.

133   W.B. Moss (1843-1927)

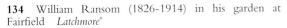

134   William Ransom (1826-1914) in his garden at Fairfield   *Latchmore*

135 William Foster and his family at Park Street, Christmas 1873

136 Frank Bowler, the Hitchin Town Crier, *c.*1860 *Latchmore*

137 Philip Allen, the Hitchin Beadle (died 1889) *Latchmore*

William Foster and three of his sons carried on the successful family carpentry and joinery business in Park Street which remained in their family till the 1920s when A.V. Duller took over.

A carpenter with a shop in Bancroft, Philip Allen, was better known as the beadle at St Mary's. He and the Town Crier Frank Bowler are representatives of jobs that have been replaced:

138 Lawson Thompson talking to the Rev. J.W. Tilt of Ickleford

in Allen's case this occurred after his death in 1889, when peelers in top hats became common.

Another character remembered with affection is Lawson Thompson, Chairman of Hitchin UDC who could yet say: 'I would rather be Chairman of the Horde of Guardians than a member of the Urban District Scoundrels.' After fifty years on High Street as a clothier and draper, he retired in 1905 after a full life involving participation in the British School, Hospital and Mechanics' Institute movements, and founding the Hitchin Savings Bank.

Lawson Thompson's garden at his Elmside home was cared for by Edward Gray, here seen in his splendid domain. Outside, law enforcement was the province of the police force, here represented by Mr. Tripp and the three generations of the Reynolds family. In 1898 Superintendent John

Reynolds became Deputy Chief Constable until he retired in 1911 after 51 years' service. Hitchin folk collected £226 as a token of their esteem for this rigid disciplinarian. His son William was chief clerk to the force for some time, retiring in 1909 after 28 years, and the grandson William John served until ill health forced him to retire after the First World War.

The group photo shows the family of the man whose work dominates this book, T.B. Latchmore. His father Thomas stands at the back behind his wife Maria, seated in her Quaker bonnet. Of his sons, Frank kept his father's grocery shop, Joseph went to Leeds as a warehouseman, George became manager of Barclays Bank in Luton, while Arthur was also in banking and was head of the local Blue Cross Temperance Brigade.

139 Thomas Latchmore and his family in the garden near Butts Close, 1873 *Latchmore*

141 Three generations of policemen in the Reynolds family, 1907

140 Mr. Tripp the policeman, *c.*1869

142 Edward Gray, the Elmside gardener

When this scion of the Hitchin Priory family retired from his parish, he was presented with a dining room clock inscribed 'Presented to the Rev. Arthur Delmé Radcliffe on resigning the Rectory of Holwell, Hitchin, as a loving memento of nine years' faithful labour and happy communion, by his affectionate parishers and friends'. He died at the early age of 46, but his son Ralph succeeded his uncle, Francis Augustus Delmé Radcliffe, at the Priory. After receiving a knighthood for political services in 1961, he died in 1963, breaking the family's link with Hitchin after over 400 years.

This same uncle F.A. Delmé Radcliffe appears in a light bowler in the group at the Conservative Club in Sun Street, the building purchased at auction in 1885 for £1,470 by the Club's Secretary, Mr. Francis Shillitoe seated on the left. Prominent amongst those celebrating his election victory, sits the ample form of the Hon. Baron Dimsdale, who was Member of Parliament for the Hitchin Division from 1885 to 1892 when ill health made him resign.

143   The Rev. Arthur Delmé Radcliffe and his family outside Holwell Rectory

144   Group photograph at the election of Baron Dimsdale, 1886

The children eyeing the camera keenly are near Portmill Lane, the home for many years of the uncrowned king of Hitchin, John Hawkins. He would probably have known them for he loved his fellow men and helped those in need, whether they were schoolboys or old ladies. Hawkins founded the Hitchin Friendly Institution and with his medical brother Frederick established the Hospital on Bedford Road. He was a well-known local solicitor and his eldest son Henry became the famous judge Lord Brampton. Apart from his many acts of benevolence, Hawkins is remembered also for his eccentricities, many of which are linked to his cart. W.O. Times in his Memoirs noted that:

… five nights a week for years with great regularity his four-wheeled dog-cart, the single horse driven by his lifelong servant Smith, could be seen proceeding to Putteridge, King's Walden Park, The Hoo or Henlow Grange or any of the other large houses. Afterwards, John would say: 'Give me the reins, Smith, I know how drunk I am, I don't know how drunk you are.'

145   Group of children and driver in Bancroft   *Latchmore*

146   John Hawkins (1791-1877) in his carriage, with Smith at the horse's head

147 Mr. Blee, the postman at St Ippollitts, 1866

Adult Sunday School and Treasurer of the Hitchin Liberal Association. Dying in 1896, he was buried in Hitchin's Quaker burial ground, leaving a son and two daughters.

The Rev. George Gainsford came to Hitchin at 23 as a curate of St Mary's to the Rev. Henry Wiles, whose daughter Annette he married in 1854. They left Hitchin that year but returned in 1863 to build and endow a new church in the station area. On Ascension Day, 1865 St Saviour's Church was consecrated, and he became its first incumbent, remaining there for 45 years. Both he and his wife did an enormous amount of good work in Hitchin, and on the occasion of both their funerals, all business in the town was suspended.

Isaac Chalkley was apprenticed as a millwright with Ransomes of Ipswich and in 1852 he and his father set up in Brand Street with a millwrighting and engineering business. He is also remembered as the Captain of the Hitchin Fire Brigade. He was a Congregationalist, unlike Dr. Oswald Foster who was a Quaker but became an Anglican on his marriage. Foster was for years the Hon. Medical Officer to the Hospital and a member of the Local Board.

148 John Carter, the landlord of *The Trooper Latchmore*

149 James Hack Tuke (1819-1896)

James Hack Tuke born in York in 1819, came to Hitchin in 1852 as a partner in the banking firm of Sharples and Co. He was also a great philanthropist, with a particular interest in the problems of poverty in the West of Ireland where he had travelled. He was the President of Hitchin's

Richard Odell, a Baptist, died in 1897 at the age of 93, having been Frederic Seebohm's coachman. He may very well have known one of Hitchin's familiar sights, Gypsy Draper, who went around playing his fiddle and accompanying this in his deep bass voice. When he was buried in

Reading, he was said to have been 105 years old. Samuel Piper the butcher was a mere 91 at his death, having lived all his life in Queen Street, 65 of them at No.8 where he died, and having been a member of the Hitchin Mechanics Provident Society for 71 years.

150 Mrs. Annette Gainsford (1833-1909), 1866 *G. Avery of Hitchin*

151 The Rev. George Gainsford (1829-1910) of St Saviour's Church

152 Isaac Chalkley (1824-1913) as Captain of the Hitchin Fire Brigade *Latchmore*

153 Dr. Oswald Foster (1808-1892)

156 Samuel Edward Piper (1825-1916), 1895

154 Richard Odell (1804-1897)

155 Gypsy Draper (1797-1902)

157 Reginald Leslie Hine (1883-1949) *Cundy, Mayfair*

It seems almost superfluous to write about Reginald Hine when his own writings have done so much to perpetuate his memory, but the basic information about his life may not be known. He was born at Newnham Hall, near Baldock, the third son of Neville Joseph Hine who followed his father in farming the land there. Reginald was educated at Grove School House, Baldock and then was coached for a time with an elder brother by the Rev. George Todd at the Vicarage at Newnham. He was then sent to Kent College, Canterbury and to the Leys Cambridge. In 1901 he was articled to the solicitor W.O. Times at the old established firm of Hawkins & Co. in Hitchin, to which he cycled eight miles there and back daily. On his marriage in 1912 to Florence Lee Pyman, they lived first at an old farmhouse at Ashwell End where his only child, a daughter, was born. They moved to Hitchin in 1917 and then to the Old Rectory at Willian. In 1936 he left Hawkins and entered into partnership in Hitchin with Reginald Hartley, which continued until his unfortunate death in 1949.

Many people will have their own memories of his stylish lectures or of his little idiosyncrasies. His obituary in the *Herts. Express* mentioned the sight of his tall unmistakable figure striding past the windows of Hitchin's Public Library and Museum, which latter he did so much to found, with some new treasure to add to the collection, and it will be evident to those who have read Hine's *Confessions of an Un-common Attorney* that he was a voracious collector. Before his death, he was working on a history of Hertfordshire, but although his name will always be associated with Hitchin, his range of writing was wide, from *Dreams and the Way of Dreams* to an article on the Duke of Monmouth's pocket-book. No-one who has read his works can doubt the most impressive breadth of his learning, but in his early days he was also a very good sportsman, playing golf, tennis and cricket—people still remember seeing him hit a six right out of the Cricket Club's ground.

Hine confessed to a soft spot for the Lucases, partly as he found an entry in William Lucas's

158 William Lucas (1804–1861) *Maull & Polyblank, Piccadilly*

diary for 1798: 'Paid 2/6 for cherries which I gave to Thomas Hine.' This William Lucas was the father of the watercolourist Samuel and the witty banker Francis, as well as of the subject of the last of the portraits in this section, also named William Lucas. He too left behind a literary work which he began at the age of 56, mainly as an antidote to ill-health, and he hoped that it would be read with interest 'in the limited circle of descendants, if not calculated for a larger audience'. This was published under the title of *A Quaker Journal* in 1934 and gives a fascinating insight into the life of one of the town's quiet but valuable citizens.

In his own words, we can follow his life as an apprentice in London from 1819 to 1825 when he trained as a chemist on the Haymarket, and worked from 9a.m. to 6p.m. six days a week. Then he faced the problem worrying the Quakers who were involved in something as questionable as brewing and says that his father 'did not wish

his sons to come into the Brewery, but the property being so much locked up in it, they could not do otherwise than continue the trade which had been in the family for more than a century'. William Lucas was therefore committed to a life at the Brewery but his journal makes it clear that he had plenty of time and energy for other activities. He was something of a poet, though not to the same extent as his brother Francis, and he also shared the family passion for nature study. He was also very much bound up with the spate of building and improvements that were going on in the town in the period around 1840—he arranged the building of the new Town Hall and assisted with the new Corn Exchange, as well as being involved with the new Quaker Meeting House on Bedford Road. His cousin Phebe (Lucas) Glaisyer describes William and his brothers as extremely well read, especially William who 'almost always had something interesting to tell us of what was going on in the literary world'.

Trades and Industries

The lie of the land has influenced much of the activity in Hitchin for the last two thousand years at least. The town lies in a valley, with gentle slopes around it, eminently suitable for the grazing of sheep; and to the north lies a tract of flat land upon which men have grown wheat and barley from time immemorial; those two basic commodities were celebrated on the old Urban District Council coat-of-arms. One of the marks of 'civilisation' is the change from a nomadic to a stationary life, consistently inhabiting one settlement and exploiting the surroundings, rather than being dominated by them.

The growing of grain crops, which in the North Hertfordshire and South Bedfordshire area has been helped by the equable climate, has been a remarkably constant factor in the history of the town, and by the 1850s the trade had become important enough to warrant the construction of a Corn Exchange. Built to the design of W. Beck, and costing just under £2,000, it opened for business on 22 March 1853.

The farmers were admitted free of charge, while the dealers paid an annual rent of up to £3 for their booths. Bakers were charged 10s. 6d. per annum and were not regarded as dealers. The dealers were not simply buying corn for milling into flour for bread, but barley for melting and brewing, and various seed-grains for oil and seed cakes for cattle-fodder. Nor were the dealers particularly local, for the booths bore the names of manufacturers and seedsmen as far afield as Stourbridge and Liverpool. This would not have been possible had the building been put up ten years earlier, for the opening of the railway three years before, in 1850, no doubt

159 (left) The interior of the Corn Exchange, *c.*1917

160 (right) Children plucking lavender blooms in Perks & Llewellyn's yard, *c.*1910 *Latchmore*

103

161 Harvesting lavender for Perks and Llewellyn, *c*.1900

162 Perks and Llewellyn's lavender still

contributed to the success of the enterprise. The new building was an immediate success, for in the year after its opening it was found necessary to improve access to the Corn Exchange by demolishing the Shambles, a building which had stood in the Market Square, directly in front of the Corn Exchange.

The lie of the land was also responsible for another local industry, the growing of lavender—rather more demanding than wheat and barley in its needs.

The name 'lavender' is derived from Latin and early Spanish words connected either with washing or with the plant's bright blue flowers. The Romans certainly used the plant for its scent in their elaborate ablutions, and the poet Virgil, who retired to Naples where it grew wild, recommended its planting near bee-hives, in order to flavour the honey.

The first record of lavender-growing in Hitchin dates from 1568, when the plant was introduced to this country from southern Europe. To grow successfully here it requires a loamy soil on a south-facing slope, shielded from the wind.

From 1823 the firm of Perks and Llewellyn, founded in 1790, specialised in the preparation of lavender products, and owned 10 major fields which satisfied the plants needs, at Mount Pleasant, Gaping Hills and Grays Lane Fields.

The lavender was propagated either by parting the roots, or by taking small cuttings in October which were then bedded out for a year. In that second October the young plants were bedded out in rows four feet apart, and then frequently manured.

Harvesting took place in the third and most productive year of the plants' growth, for by the fourth year they became too 'woody' for convenient use. The blooms were cut by hand with sickles

and taken back to the firm's High Street premises, where girls cut off the stalks, whose presence in the still degraded the end product.

The distillation was not without its hazards, and not from the most obvious sources. 'Great care is needed on the part of those who handle the sheaves ... to guard against being stung by the bees which remain attached to the flowers ... hundreds are thrown into the still ... in a state of hopeless intoxication.'

Perks and Llewellyn's still was quite small, and directly heated by a fire underneath, and rival firms were always ready to point out how this could affect the results. T.J. Barnett, who made lavender oil at his premises in Sun Street remarked: 'The heating the stills by steam possesses many advantages over the naked fire, as by the former process the Lavender has no chance of getting burned or the Oil obtaining an empyreumatic odour through the application of too great a heat.' Perks and Llewellyn used an open fire, nonetheless, and distilled very slowly; it took about four hours to deal with a still-full, and consequently it took nearly three weeks to distil a year's harvest, for in a good year the fields would yield up to 30lb. per acre. After distillation, the essential oil which resulted was collected over water, on which it floated, and then bottled. It was left for four years to mature in the bottles. To make lavender water, the essential oil was blended with up to forty times its own volume of spirit.

Lavender water was not the sole product of Perks and Llewellyn: they also manufactured a range of soaps and toiletries. 'The Series of Lavender Bloom Shaving and Toilet Soaps sent out by Messrs. Perks are in truth really unique ... immeasurably superior to any others we have tested.' This comment, from the *War Office Times and Naval Review*

163 Mr. Perks's shop on High Street, 10 March, 1863

164 The interior of Perks and Llewellyn's shop, 1959 From *The Chemist and Druggist*

of 1907, is typical of the acclaim accorded the firm's products. This was true abroad too: Perks and Llewellyn were given an Honourable Mention at the International Exhibition of 1862, were awarded a Prize Medal at the Paris Exhibition of 1867, and the Medal, Diploma and Report of the Philadelphia International Exhibition of 1876, whose catalogue said of lavender 'There are now about 35 acres of land in Hitchin devoted to its culture, yielding sufficient essential oil to produce upwards of 2,000 gallons of lavender water annually'. The rising cost of labour eventually caused the industry to decline, and commercial production has now ceased in the Hitchin area.

Willow suitable for basketry grows best on soft, marshy ground, and such ground existed for many years at the north end of Bancroft where the Recreation Ground now stands. This was surely not the only area in the neighbourhood where such willow grew, for during the latter half of the last century the town supported four or five basketmakers.

Willow for basketry is first harvested in the winter of its third year of growth, and is cut off close to the ground with a sharp billhook. The harvesting of the withies is the only stage of the preparatory process which is not shown in the photograph of the Bancroft osier bed, but William Beaver, who had a basketmaking shop in Swan Yard, off the Market Place, is standing beside a bundle of harvested withies.

On the right, four youths are pulling the withies through iron 'brakes', whose blades pinched the withies and peeled back the bark.

In the foreground, Mr. Abbiss is fastening the peeled withies in a clamp, ready for bundling into the standard bundle of 37 in. circumference. Once bundled, the peeled withies are ready for the basketmaker, and on the left James Bullard stands with a bundle, ready to take it away to his shop in the Churchyard. The Bullard family had long been basketmakers, for in 1839 one Richard had worked at his craft in a shop in Bancroft, and the James Bullard in the photograph was succeeded by his son James. The family business in the Churchyard ceased trade in 1913 on the death of the younger James.

The basketmaker uses few tools in his craft, largely because his hands are the best tools he could have, despite the toughness of the withies. He uses a 'cleaver' to split a withy into three or four narrower 'skeins', and small shoe-like 'shavers' to pare a withy into an even width along its length. A pointed bodkin, for parting the weave, and a small knife complete the craftsman's toolkit.

George Day's basketry shop in Tilehouse Street was until recently a well-known local landmark. George's death around 1955 severed a living link with the photograph of the Bancroft osier-bed, for George's father had been apprenticed to the William Beaver who appears in the photograph. Basketry, however, was—and still is—a craft which satisfies a limited need, for durable containers. Fashion, on the other hand, is fickle, and can make vast demands upon resources, but that demand may die away very rapidly. Fashion dictated that straw bonnets and hats were *de rigueur* in the last century, and it was only the styles which changed over many years. Straw-plaiting furnished the straw-hat makers of Luton and elsewhere with their basic material. First recorded in Hitchin in 1630, the plaiting process became so

lucrative to its practitioners by the 19th century that in some cases men abandoned farm labouring, as they could make more money by straw-plaiting, but in general it was women and children who made most of the plait. Children were taught the process at home and then sent out to plaiting schools, sometimes before their fourth birthday; the function of the schoolmistress was to ensure the children fulfilled their daily quota. Frequently the mistress could not read, and the other schools were known as 'reading schools' to underline the distinction.

The process itself began when a farmer sold straw to a dealer, who combed it with an iron comb to straighten it and remove the stem-leaves, and made up bundles of 56, 80 or 112 lbs. The bundles were then bleached with sulphur fumes, and dyed, if required. After being sorted through a series of wire sieves, the straws were made up into bundles for sale in the Market Square to the plaiters.

The plaiter chose straws of the size suitable for the type of work required, tied them into a small bundle, tucked them under her left arm and set to work. The various patterns were made with up to seven 'ends' or straws and as each individual straw was only nine or ten inches long, new straws were set in at regular intervals. Early plait is termed 'wholestraw' as the whole straw was used, but as demand grew for finer work the 'strawsplitter' was developed to split a straw along its length into up to nine 'splints'. Splints enabled fine plait to be made, comparable to the expensive Italian imports. After flattening in a 'plait mill' with grooved wooden rollers, the plait was ready for sale to the Luton hatmakers' representatives.

Two major factors account for the decline of the straw-plait industry in North Hertfordshire and the adjacent areas—the 1870 Education Act and the repeal of import duty on plait in 1861.

The plaiting schools were abolished under the Education Act and thus deprived the industry of its cheapest labour, but this in itself need not have been a death-blow. The repeal of import duty was, however, and by 1869 Chinese Canton plait was being imported in sufficient quantities to be a threat. In 1874 a Plait Hall was built in Hollow Lane to serve as a market, but it was already too late; the building was sold in 1898 and subsequently became St Andrew's Mission Church. Despite attempts to revive it in the 1890s, the industry was dead. Those who still plaited knew no other skill, had plaited all their lives and felt that 'they might as well do that as nothing, and that after all, the good old days may come back'. Apart from the abortive Plait Hall in Hollow Lane, which still stands, the industry left few traces.

165 (above) George Day's basket shop in Tilehouse Street   *Latchmore*

166 (right) A girl demonstrating straw-plaiting, *c.*1907

167 (bottom) The Bancroft osier-bed, 1877   *Latchmore*

168 Odell's Carriage Repository *Latchmore*

In his diary, William Lucas (the father of Samuel Lucas the watercolourist) records on 1 December 1822, the death of Thomas Odell, a blacksmith. Pigot's 1839 Directory lists three blacksmiths called Odell in the Hitchin area; Jephtha in Pirton, Thomas in Bridge Street in Hitchin, and John close by in Bucklersbury.

The same directory lists 10 other blacksmiths in the Hitchin area, reflecting the importance of the trade in a rural community. The horse was still the only mobile form of power available for personal transport and heavy agricultural work and needed frequent re-shoeing, as road surfaces all too often left much to be desired. The usual method of road maintenance was to plough it up twice a year, and lay down a foundation of faggots. On top of this was laid soil, bricks, gravel and flints. Although faggots were a common foundation, anything might suffice in times of necessity; bullocks' horns were used on occasion in Hitchin Market Place, as well

as stones from the old Priory buildings, and a fully harnessed dead horse was once used to fill a particularly deep rut in Brand Street.

On these varied surfaces, horseshoes wore out quickly, and the blacksmiths were kept busy. The smiths were capable of working iron for any purpose, however, and made or repaired any item in the vast range of farm equipment, from the humble spade to the plough.

Early on, there had been little difference between the blacksmith and the farrier, or shoeing-smith, but as time went on, men tended to specialise into one field or the other, but the demarcation line was very vague. In 1855, Robert Odell called himself a farrier, but by 1878 he called himself a shoeing and general smith and worked in what is now 32 Bridge Street. By this time, the family had diversified the business and another member of the family, also called Robert, was operating further down Bridge Street as a carriage builder.

169 A Sanders bus body, destined for a local route

The family had been Baptists for generations, and when Robert the younger discovered his son Walter reading a harmless boys' magazine, he cast the child out of the house. Some years later Robert discovered his son was serving in the Royal Horse Artillery, and suitably contrite, he bought the boy out. Walter set up in Portmill Lane as a coachbuilder, but by 1894 he had given up those premises and returned to Bridge Street as part of Odell Brothers. Another Robert Odell was a shoeing smith in Bridge Street, and a Stephen Odell was a plain smith in Bucklersbury.

The Odell family continued their intimate involvement with carriages and horses until 1898, when they were bought out by Ralph E. Sanders and Son.

Ralph Sanders had announced the opening of his business in Royston with an advertisement in the August 1876 issue of the *Royston Crow* in which he begged 'to solicit public patronage, which it will

be his constant endeavour to deserve'. The Hitchin Directory of 1902 described his firm as 'Carriage builders, cycle manufacturers and motor car engineers', and this accurately reflects the development of their business.

Those who could afford it had always had their own carriages—William Ransom can be seen with his carriage later in this chapter, and one or two others appear elsewhere in this book—and the less wealthy might possess a dog-cart or perhaps a governess car. Gottlieb Daimler's invention of the petrol engine, and Karl Benz's first commercially available motor car of 1888 found most orthodox carriagemakers rather puzzled or confused. Used to producing straightforward wooden structures perfectly adequate for the stresses resulting from a horse's trotting speed, they were now called upon to build vehicles capable of withstanding up to twice the speed over the same indifferent road surfaces, pushed

170   A Sanders pony-phaeton

along from underneath rather than drawn from the
front. Not only that, they had to endure the vibra-
tion produced by a poorly mounted, low-revving
engine.

The carriage-builders' response to these demands
was at first to produce a simple adaptation of the
traditional coach. This can be seen by comparing
the photograph of William Ransom's coach with
that of the Sanders-built car body. The car engine
has been mounted over the front wheels, while the
driver's seat retains its original position, being
lowered and provided with a simple cab and wind-
screen.

The method of manufacture was also the same.
The photograph of Sanders' workshop shows on the
left several men building the traditional dog-carts
and governess cars, while on the right, against the
light, stands an incomplete car body, built by the
same staff in the same workshop. In front of the car,
a man is adjusting the tyre on a wooden wheel with
a large gear fitted to its axle—a car back wheel
identical to the 'cart'-wheels standing around the
workshop.

Other extant photographs of the workshop show
car bodies being assembled by the traditional 'coach'
methods, and with the same materials, wood, glue,
and clamps, In the same way, the car bodies are
assembled among the half-finished carts.

This transitional stage of car manufacture, an
engineering firm supplying the engine and
transmission and coachbuilders supplying the bodywork mainly to special order, was to last for several
years until mass-production of metal bodies became
common.

In the course of time, many small firms which
had produced car bodies to order found their trade
being supplanted by the large-scale manufacturers'
products, and either closed down or specialised in
selling the mass-produced car. Sanders and Son were
no exception to this trend, eventually closing down
their bodywork department to concentrate on repairs and selling.

The firm built elaborate premises, Hitchin's first
brick-built motor garage in Walsworth Road in 1906,
which it occupied until the business was sold in
1979.

171   A Sanders four-wheeled dog-cart

172   A Sanders body on a French chassis

173 Sanders' coachbuilding workshop

Virtually from the moment he discovered the nutritional value of grain, man must also have discovered the interesting side-effects of fermented barley.

Because it is so close to an extensive barley growing area, Hitchin has always had many taverns and hostelries, and ample breweries to sustain them, the most notable being that founded by the Lucas family in 1709. Early on in its history, the Lucases were in partnership with a brother-in-law, one Isaac Gray, but eventually the Lucas family took over completely. In 1783, when William Lucas made a settlement on his marriage to Susanna Camps, his property was described in the deeds as: 'All that capital messuage or Tenement ... in Hitchin in a certain street there called Angel Street ... all those barns, outhouses, edifices, and all that yard with the Malthouse, Brewhouse and other houses there erected ...'. Angel Street was the old name for Sun Street, and the Lucas brewery was to do business on the same site for the whole of the firm's lifetime.

By 1897, when the firm's Bitter Ale cost 1s. per gallon, and India Pale Ale 1s. 6d., the brewery site contained a mineral water factory, cask and bottle-washing department, cooperage, and workshops for carpenters and engineers, as well as the buildings for the production and storage of beer. In 1896 the firm became a limited company, W. & S. Lucas Ltd., as can be seen from the beer-bottles of the period.

Samuel Lucas the elder in his childhood had promised to indulge his passion for painting only in his spare time from running the family firm, but he achieved a prodigious output of watercolours and sketches nonetheless. His son, Samuel the younger, born in 1840, followed in his father's footsteps and expanded his interest in brewing to include Barnsley Brewery, Messrs. Parker of Burslem and several breweries in Chicago, Milwaukee and New York. He broke with tradition when he ceased membership of the Quakers to become an Anglican, and married the daughter of the United States Consul at Leeds.

After his death in 1919 the brewery was beset with the same problems that afflicted many small businesses at the time: increased labour costs, post-war inflation, and the very dry weather of the early 1920s which may well have caused insuperable problems to a process which relied heavily upon water. By 1923, the buildings were in a sorry state, and they were finally replaced in 1963.

174 The Lucas Brewery yard, 1876 *Nichols*

175   Newtons' joinery workshop

176   Newton's staff casting lead for repairs to the roof of
St Mary's Church

177   A Newtons advertisement in a local magazine

It has long been the custom to record the names of churchwardens who have effected repairs or improvements to a church in the lead on the roof, and St Mary's is no exception, for the roof bears the inscriptions: 1775—John Coulson, Plumber; 1813—R. & I. Newton; 1840—T. & R. Newton; 1907—(on the tower) F. Newton; 1909—(on the north side) F. Newton.

These bald statements record the bare basics of the history of one of the longest-running firms in Hitchin. The firm had been established some time before 1676 by members of the Coulson family, and in 1686 a Thomas Coulson was elected a Churchwarden of the town. The Churchwardens were members of the Vestry, which constituted the 'Local Government' of the time, and only citizens of some repute and prosperity were elected. Two generations later, in 1776, John Coulson apprenticed his nephew Robert Newton. The young Robert was enjoined to serve his master for seven years, 'his secrets keep, his lawful commands everywhere gladly do … Taverns, Inns or Alehouses he shall not haunt. At Cards, Dice, Tables, or any other unlawful Games, he shall not play nor contract Matrimony Fornication nor from the service of his said Master Day or Night absent himself …' On the death of John Coulson Robert Newton took over the business and ran it under his own name. He himself became a Churchwarden in 1803, a post which he held until 1825. In 1810 he took his son Isaac into partnership and the firm continued as 'Newton and Son, Painters, Plumbers and Glaziers'.

Isaac Newton ran the firm after his father's death in 1836, and his success and popularity in connection with the town's Fire Brigade is discussed in the appropriate chapter, for the firm had been responsible for the storage and upkeep of the appliances since 1804. Isaac was also responsible for the appliances at Offley, where he and his father had releaded the church roof in 1814.

On his death in 1859 Isaac was succeeded by his son Thomas, who forged a link with another long-standing local firm by marrying into the Gatward family. Thomas's son Francis, who was born in 1863, nearly disrupted the family's association with the business, for after his apprenticeship in Hertford and a brief spell in Bedford, he almost resolved not to work in Hitchin, but thought better of it. He went into partnership with his brother Edgar for a few years and expanded the business until it had over three hundred employees. He became a member of the Local Board (the body which preceded the Urban District Council) and was responsible for many improvements to the town's water supply and sewage disposal systems.

After the death of Francis Newton in 1922, the business suffered a decline in the hands of Francis's two sons Basil and George, and five years later two of the employees, Harry Day and T.H. Coleman bought the firm. They and their descendants have successfully administered the firm ever since.

178   Work about to start on the cinema in the Market Place which opened in 1913

179   William Ransom with his brougham, *c.*1907   *Latchmore*

180   Ransom's staff harvesting belladonna

Another notable member of the Quaker fraternity was William Ransom, founder of the firm of pharmaceutical chemists in Bancroft. Born in the family farm at the north end of Bancroft in 1826, the young William was sent to study at Isaac Brown's Academy, where he met Joseph Lister, later to become Lord Lister, Birket Foster, who later became a watercolourist of some repute, and Joseph Pollard, later a noted botanist. The talents of his friends and the guidance of his teacher obviously influenced a lively mind, and fortunately William's parents were wise enough to allow him to pursue his scientific interests, apprenticing him to Southalls of Birmingham, a firm of manufacturing chemists.

After he had qualified in pharmacy, William returned to Hitchin and set up his own business in 1846 in the premises which the firm still occupies. By 1858, his labours had brought him due credit and he was able to marry Anna Mary Southall, the eldest daughter of Thomas Southall to whom he had been apprenticed.

Pharmaceutical chemistry was by no means the limit of his scientific pursuits, for he was a Fellow of the Society of Antiquaries, having excavated Pegsdon tumulus and Purwell's Roman villa, and he was also Fellow of the Linnaean and Numismatic Societies. He was as devoted to the town as to science, and served on many committees, was a Director of the Market Company and the Gas Company, became a justice of the Peace and served on the County Council.

The results of William's experiments with an old copper still, which his grandmother had used for distilling sweet herbs, gained him a Prize Medal at the International Exhibition of 1862.

Four years later William closed down the retail side of the business in order to concentrate on pharmaceutical chemistry—the preparation of the basic elements of medicines. Some of the plants which he studied he was able to grow first at the family farm in Bancroft and later at Bearton Farm, plants such as Henbane, Wild Lettuce and Belladonna. Others had to be imported from as far afield as Syria. Still others grew wild in the fields around the town and were collected by Hitchin people, mostly those who lived in the Queen Street slums. This applied particularly to dandelion roots which were always collected immediately after harvest, but the demolition of the slums dispersed the collectors, and the advent of power-assisted farm machinery meant that the field could be reploughed so soon after harvest that there was no time to dig for dandelion roots. Before this custom collapsed in the early 1930s, as much as twenty tons of the roots might be brought into the distillery on a Saturday morning.

In 1913, the firm became a limited company with a capital of £30,000. William Ransom died in 1914 and was succeeded by his only son Francis, who had passed his pharmacy examinations in 1883 and become his father's partner two years later. He began research on familiar drugs, which in particular led to a revolution in the galenical preparations of Belladonna. He was elected President of the Pharmaceutical Society in 1910 and was also renowned in Hitchin for owning the first bicycle in the town to be fitted with pneumatic tyres.

The firm grew lavender, as may be seen in the photograph, but it was not grown in competition with Perks and Llewellyn, but for refining its medicinal properties. However, Ransom's did refine lavender for use in toiletries after Perks and Llewellyn had closed down. Ransom's has been notable for the devotion of its staff, for it has been common for several members of the same family to work there, and many have worked there for the greater part of their lives: Alfred Latchmore (the nephew of T.B. Latchmore the photographer) worked for Ransom's, as did his daughter Aillie who started in 1915 and left 43 years later. Others have worked fifty years or more, and Arthur Foster was in his 67th year with the firm when he died, aged 79.

The firm became a public company in 1969, and exports a wide range of drugs to many countries; a catalogue lists agencies in 49 countries from the Arabian Gulf to Venezuela.

Ransom's no longer run any farms in the Hitchin area, but maintain about four hundred acres for drug-growing at Wiggin Hill near St Ives in Huntingdonshire.

181   Ransom's lavender fields

182   Cutting peppermint

Another Hitchin industry which owes its existence to the shape of the landscape is tanning, for without the hillsides there would be few sheep, and without the sheep—and cows—there would be no hides to tan. The presence of a reliable watercourse is also essential.

Even in Palaeolithic times man saw the value of the hides of animals for clothing, and for a host of other useful appurtenances such as water-bags or foot-coverings, and knew how to scrape, dry and oil the skins, to make them most useful. Homer described how a hide could be cleaned and then impregnated with fats and greases to retain its suppleness, and the basics of the process have changed little since then.

Leather is required to have different properties for different purposes: a shoe, for example, needs a soft, flexible leather on the upper to allow the foot to bend, while the sole requires a thick leather of great toughness to protect the soft sole of the foot from stones, and the tanning process can be adjusted to produce leather with different characteristics.

Hides arrive at a tannery direct from the slaughterhouse and require extensive cleaning before they can be tanned, and the preparatory process is termed 'fellmongering'. It is known that fellmongering was carried on in Hitchin before 1775 by the predecessors of John Whiting on a site not far from the Biggin.

The hides were soaked in pits of gently moving clean water, which removed the dried blood on the skin and caused the fibres to swell up. After this, a

183   Russell's tanyard in Bancroft, *c.*1880

184 A lime-trough in Russell's tannery *P. Blair Ferguson*

soaking in lime-pits loosened the hair on the surface which could then be cut off with a knife. A further soaking in clean water allowed the residue of fat to be removed with the long, two-handled 'fleshing-knife' which is depicted on the town's coat-of-arms.

At this point the tanning process proper could begin. By the beginning of the 19th century, Whiting's tannery had moved to Bancroft, and in 1866 G.W. Russell and Henry Featherstone took over from Joseph Whiting and the firm grew to include the associated trades of leather-dressing and parchment manufacture.

The aim of tanning is to fill the leather with tannin, which inhibits its decay. The tannin was obtained from oak-bark, which was ground to a dust and mixed with cold water; the time the hides spent in this liquor and the earlier limepits determined the properties of the leather. The hides started off in a weak liquor, and were moved into pits of increasing strength until the fibres were absolutely saturated, a process which might take up to six weeks. The saturated hides were quickly washed, oiled with crude cod liver oil and allowed to dry slowly.

After rolling, which knitted the fibres tightly together, the hides were dry and stiff, ready for the currier. His task was to clean the leather of all traces of dried tanning liquor which clogged the grain, which he did with a flat steel blade, or 'sleaker'. To

185 Making parchment in Russell's tannery *P. Blair Ferguson*

restore the suppleness of the hide and to make it, waterproof it had to be 'stuffed' with various fats and greases, such as dubbin. Modern technology has improved the stuffing process over the last 90 years, but the essentials of the process remain the same. In 1886 the partnership of Russell and Featherstone was dissolved, and the firm of G.W. Russell and Son was formed. In 1949 Russells bought the business of E. & J. Richardson of Newcastle, and by so doing secured the sole manufacturing rights for fine book-binding leathers; it was a Russells leather which bound the Queen's Bible at her Coronation in 1953.

Although reference has already been made to barley with respect to brewing, the town contained more maltings than were necessary to supply the local breweries. This was no accident, for the majority of the maltings supplied the London breweries. This caused problems, for the heavy wagons furrowed and tore up the roads; in the early 17th century the local magistrates attempted to have the malt transferred to pack-horses, but the trade was so lucrative that their protests were to no avail.

The malting process in itself is quite simple, but the skill lies in producing consistent results. William Lucas the brewer owned a copy of Thomas Tryon's *New Art of Brewing Beer, Ale and other Sort of Liquors*, which remarks of the soaking (which causes the grain to germinate) 'if the Weather be warm two days and three nights may do ... but in Winter ... five or six will do it no harm ...'. After draining, it is heaped on the malthouse floor and frequently turned over. The time from soaking until the roasting in the kiln, which stops the germination, varies according to the weather from three to five weeks. Tryon recommends a very light roasting: 'Now as to Barley, God and his Handmaid Nature have ... indued it with that moft amiable Colour, White ... therefore in your Preparation ... ufe all Art and Means to maintain it, for the whiter your drink is, the better and more Healthful.'

The consequences of over-roasting are dire, for the resulting beer is highly coloured, and 'its natural Operation in the Body is to heat the Blood, deftroying Appetite, obstructs the Stomach, sending grofs dulling Fumes into the Head, ... dulls the fine pure Spirits, hinders the free circulation of the Blood by Stagnating the Humours, and in the Cholerick and Melancholy Complexions generates the Stone, Gravel, Gout and Confumption.' One trusts William Lucas took note.

The only maltings which was still known by name when all the others had been forgotten was the Wratten, which stood at the corner of Wratten Road and Charlton Road. Demolished in 1970, an office block now occupies the site.

186 The Wratten Maltings in the 1930s *Latchmore*

The Good Old Days ...

The Public Health Act of 1848 permitted local authorities, on the submission of a petition of one-tenth of the inhabitants, to hold an enquiry into the state of public health there. This Hitchin undertook most promptly, appointing one William Ranger to examine the situation. His findings were published by Her Majesty's Stationery Office in a slim pamphlet in 1849.

The population of Hitchin was growing rapidly in the early years of the 19th century. The 1831 census listed 5,211 inhabitants, and that for 1841, 6,125, an increase of almost one-sixth in 10 years. This growth was largely due not to an overall increase in population, but to people moving from the countryside into towns, largely as a result of increased mechanisation.

There was little apparent attempt to cater directly for this influx. The majority found accommodation, but it was mostly hastily built.

Mr. Foster, surgeon, stated that the most prevalent character of the disease among the poorer class during the last 12 months has been typhoid and scarlet fever; that out of 1,700 cases of sickness, from 800 to 900 were those of fever. In the autumn of 1848, the medical officer of the Union had no less than 100 cases of fever under treatment at one time; and the number of deaths from its malignancy in one year, i.e. from April 1848 to April 1849, amounted to 71, or about 1 in 12; it generally occurred where filth abounded. One of the first cases that attracted his attention occurred in a locality where an extensive privy-pit existed; the soil flowed down upon the surface of the yard, added to collections of horse manure for public sale.

Ranger's survey gives a frightening account of the overcrowding at the time, the following examples are given as illustrative:

In Davis's—alley, containing 7 houses, a family, consisting of 7 persons, occupy one small room, without any outlet at back or means of ventilation, for sleeping.

Chapman's Yard contains 17 houses, without any outlets at back, reached by means of a covered passage. The number of persons in 6 of these houses varies from 7 to 10 in each, and in one, a man, with 4 children, occupy one small room for sleeping; a girl, 16 years of age, sleeping with three of her brothers; the eldest 18.

Carter's Yard contains 4 houses, but no outlet at back; in one of these, a family of 10 persons reside, i.e. man, wife and 8 children; having only one small sleeping room 12 feet by 11 feet by 7 feet; the three eldest consisting of a girl, boy and girl, of the respective ages of 21, 20 and 16 years, the fourth, also a girl, 14 years of age.

Ranger had clearly seen similar conditions elsewhere, since he then turns his attention directly to the water supply and the drainage arrangements.

The inhabitants at present obtain their supply of water ... from draw-wells, by means of pumps, and from the river. The total number of pumps in the town, public and private, is estimated at 357, and of wells 92 ... but those residing on the sides of the river avail themselves of the latter source by dipping: the dipping-place itself being in close proximity to privies and outfalls of drains.

The privy accommodation for 5,176 of the inhabitants, residing in 1,057 houses, may be classed under 4 heads:

1. Houses without any convenience
2. Houses with *boxes*
3. With open privies
4. With water-closets

In Corries'-Yard there are five privies with soil-pits, for the use of 109 persons; the drains pass through one of these privies, which is described by one of the inhabitants as frequently overflowing, the soil being swilled into the street.

In Bridge Street there are 20 privies to 31 houses; the soil from 14 is deposited in cess-pools, from 6 it is discharged into river, near to where the inhabitants abstract water for drinking and domestic purposes: but three of the houses are destitute of privy accommodation of any kind. In Chapman's Yard there are 2 privies to 17 houses occupied by 90 persons; the soil is discharged into the river, over which the two privies are built.

Mr. Newton stated that the present cost of erecting water-closets, of which there are about 59 in the town, for plumber's work alone amounts to £10, and for wood-work £3 to £5 more, and for repairs about 5 shillings annually.

The attitude of the inhabitants to unpleasant smells seems to have been one of dislike, coupled with a reluctance to do anything about it. The high density of population, coupled with the density of activity, meant that all kinds of waste went astray.

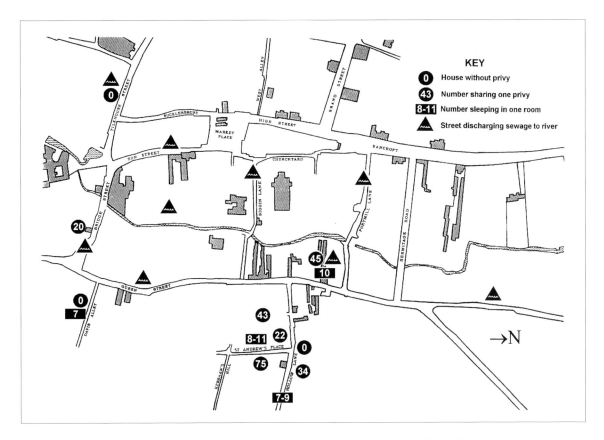

KEY

0 — House without privy

43 — Number sharing one privy

8-11 — Number sleeping in one room

▲ — Street discharging sewage to river

In Parker's Yard, Bucklersbury, there is a farm-yard, and slaughter-house, with a pool of stagnant water, receiving the most valuable portion of drainage from dung; and a second farm-yard and slaughter-house in Parcell's Yard ... Hall's Yard is ... one of the seats of typhus fever. Pigs are kept on these premises, and the smell arising from slaughter-house offal and the dung is offensive to the inhabitants residing in the vicinity, more particularly when the dung is removed.

... In the early part of the year 1837 [the River Hiz] was a nuisance rather than a benefit, and calculated to injure the health of the inhabitants residing on its banks, in consequence of that part of the stream which lies above the Mill (the Port Mill in Portmill Lane) being constantly filled up with 'mud, road drift, filth and the various contents of the drains and sewers, any by rubbish occasionally thrown into it by the inhabitants of the banks' many of whom have no other means at present of disposing of the offal, etc. from their houses.

Ranger goes on to describe reports of the state of the river itself, which has filled up with mud and other unpleasantness, varying in depth from 6 inches to 4 feet between the bridge in Bridge Street and the mill-head at Port Mill lane, a distance of about 1,200 feet. 'The effect has been to raise the waterline considerably above its ancient level, and to inundate

or otherwise render the buildings, consisting chiefly of dwelling-houses, exceedingly damp ...'

The report concluded by recommending nine points of action. These were:

1. For securing to the inhabitants an abundant supply of water on the constant system filtered and carried into every tenement for domestic use, cleansing and household purposes.

2. For abolishing all cesspools and privy pits, and for draining systematically every part of the district by means of efficient tubular drains, including the houses, courtyard areas and roads.

3. For rendering the sewage and manure of the town productive by applying it by irrigation or otherwise to adjacent lands.

4. For placing fire-plugs [hydrants] throughout the town and supplies of water kept on by night as well as by day for the better extinction of fires and for street cleansing.

5. For converting existing privies into water-closets, and where neither privies nor water-closets exist erecting water closets.

6. For filling up stagnant ponds, ditches, and other receptacles for filth.

7. For insuring a complete system of ventilation of lodging-houses and for regulating the number of persons sleeping in them.

8. For paving the courts, & etc., and for the daily cleansing of the carriage- and foot-ways by the application of water, so as to prevent the accumulations of mud and filth.

9. For purchasing and removing the mill situate in the town about 1,200 feet below the bridge in Bridge Street, and for deepening the bed of the river, and excluding from the latter every kind of filth, sewage, etc.

These recommendations were faultless. He also recommended that a Local Board of Health be elected under the Public Health Act, to consist of 12 persons, re-electable annually. But that was not the end of the story at all. The gory details of the next 21 years have been recorded elsewhere, but the essentials of the tale are that the new water mains leaked, the pumping engine broke down often, and remedies bankrupted the townspeople's elected representatives. Since any new member of the Vestry, as the Council was then called, would have been responsible for the debts of the former Vestry, no-one was willing to stand. The water supply and sewerage system hobbled along under public subscription and philanthropy until central government expunged the debt, and elections could again take place.

The 1881 Hitchin Census

The conditions in Hitchin were probably little worse than in many other places. Comparing the 1881 census, over thirty years after Ranger's survey, with figures from the most recent census for Hertfordshire as a whole, 1991, the difference in conditions is marked—as it should be. This table shows the percentage of the population in each age-band.

Age	Herts 1991	Hitchin 1881
16–19	6.62	12.76
20–24	9.1	13.64
25–29	10.08	9.36
30–34	9.68	10.92
35–39	8.71	9.70
40–44	9.68	8.27
45–49	8.04	7.89
50–54	6.95	7.31
55–59	6.7	5.77
60–64	6.33	4.85
65–70	5.75	3.73
70+	12.36	5.79

The most obvious difference is in longevity—only 5.79 per cent of the 1881 population passed 70 years of age, whilst in Hertfordshire today more than double achieve this—almost one-eighth of the population. In total, 38.4 per cent of the 1881 population was under 16—when this was the segment of the population least equipped to deal with virulent bacterial infections, the replacement level was high. In addition there was no reliable method of birth control.

The population of the town in 1881 was employed in a large range of activities, though some were very small in terms of the number of people involved. The chart shows how 'scholars'—those nominally at school and not in employment—constituted the greatest single element, 34 per cent of the whole population. The 1991 Census takes little account of the economic activity of people under 16, as today there are effective legal controls in place. This was not the case in 1881, when 28 per cent of 13 year-olds were employed, 39.6 per cent at 14. Few went into service at this age—only 15 per cent of those styling themselves 'domestic servant' were under 16.

Non-agricultural labourers and strawplait workers made up 24 per cent of the whole population, and those in domestic service—cooks, maids, housemaids, butlers, footmen, valets—made up another 8 per cent. Thus 32 per cent were unskilled or low-skilled, and 34 per cent were nominally still at school, 66 per cent of the population. The remaining 34 per cent exercised the skills common to all towns, as well as those particular to Hitchin.

Analysis of census figures is beset with pitfalls, largely because of the danger of double counting those who list themselves as having more than one occupation. Many do so, making for some strange admixtures: bricklayer and music teacher, Baptist minister and baker, hairdresser and taxidermist and, perhaps most sadly and self-demeaningly, Barlow's wife. Interestingly, the industries for which the town has become well known, its brewing and tanning, feature little in the bigger picture. The lavender industry doesn't show up because the numbers involved were minute—effectively one chemist and his family, and some seasonal workers.

All the food manufacturing and retail activities combined take up 6 per cent of the population, barely more than that devoted to clothes assembly, dress makers and seamstresses, though this does not include boot and shoe makers. Female clothing manufacture was clearly very important.

Several published studies of the plait industry suggest that the industry was dying after 1874 because of imports of Chinese plait. In 1881 it seems far from moribund, with 689 people involved in it, of whom none describes themselves as 'unemployed plaiter'. Two describe themselves as 'strawplaiter, unemployed servant'. Since there is no apparent reluctance to use the term 'unemployed', we must assume that those who do not use it are in work, that nearly 700 people were still employed in plaiting, and that reports of the industry's demise were therefore premature. Only 11 per cent of those described as working with straw are under 16, with the two youngest being 7 and 8.

The railway was a major employer, keeping over 4 per cent of the town in work. The photograph of the station staff on p.72 gives an indication of the numbers involved, and this doesn't include the non-uniformed staff, track-layers, wheel-tappers, stokers, car-men, carriage-examiners and all the other niches in the vast organisation.

Only 16 of the inhabitants suggest that they are involved with chemistry or drug manufacture, and this includes businesses other than Ransom's, so here too there were presumably a number of seasonal staff, as well as those recorded as simply bringing in raw materials, such as dandelion roots, and being paid by weight for their trouble.

The tannery registers above 1 per cent of the towns workforce: there was a wide diversity of occupations—fellmongers, skinners, tanners and administrative staff, and like the railways, the operation was labour-intensive.

Mechanisation and globalisation have radically changed the make-up of the town. The railway now employs a handful of people in Hitchin. Tanning and brewing have ceased, because of the economies of scale that can be achieved by concentrating activity in just a few places. Strawplaiting is no longer conducted commercially in this country (Spanish sombreros on sale in Torremolinos are made in China). Other industries have adapted to keep up with the times: wheelwrights and blacksmiths have become car-mechanics and panel-beaters, and horse-dealers have become car-dealers. And now a significant proportion of Hitchin inhabitants don't even work in the town, since mobility is widespread, and North Hertfordshire has the highest *per capita* car ownership in the UK.

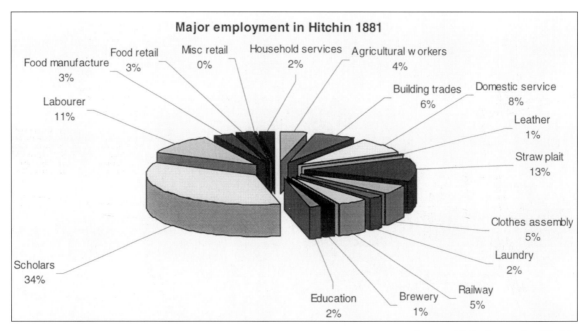

Source: 1881 Census for Hitchin

Central Hitchin

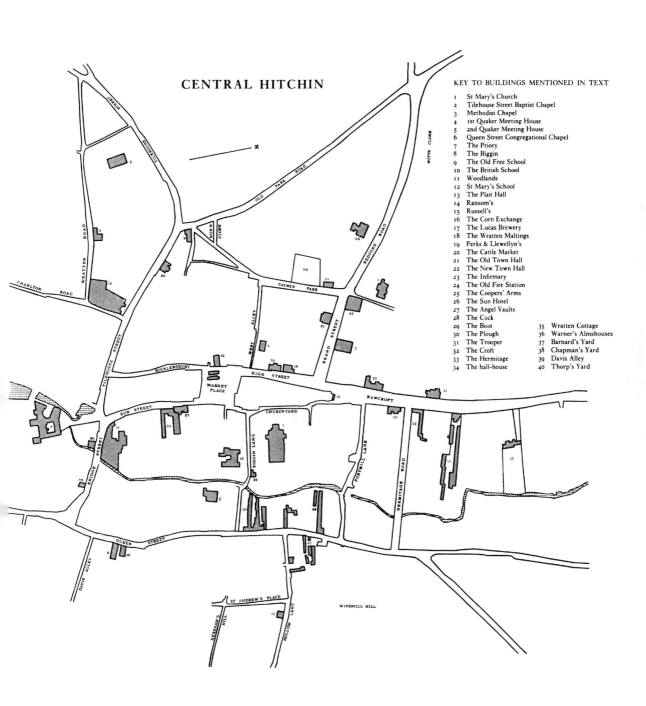

CENTRAL HITCHIN

KEY TO BUILDINGS MENTIONED IN TEXT

1 St Mary's Church
2 Tilehouse Street Baptist Chapel
3 Methodist Chapel
4 1st Quaker Meeting House
5 2nd Quaker Meeting House
6 Queen Street Congregational Chapel
7 The Priory
8 The Biggin
9 The Old Free School
10 The British School
11 Woodlands
12 St Mary's School
13 The Plait Hall
14 Ransom's
15 Russell's
16 The Corn Exchange
17 The Lucas Brewery
18 The Wratten Maltings
19 Perks & Llewellyn's
20 The Cattle Market
21 The Old Town Hall
22 The New Town Hall
23 The Infirmary
24 The Old Fire Station
25 The Coopers' Arms
26 The Sun Hotel
27 The Angel Vaults
28 The Cock
29 The Boot   35 Wratten Cottage
30 The Plough   36 Warner's Almshouses
31 The Trooper   37 Barnard's Yard
32 The Croft   38 Chapman's Yard
33 The Hermitage   39 Davis Alley
34 The hall-house   40 Thorp's Yard

Hitchin and its Surroundings

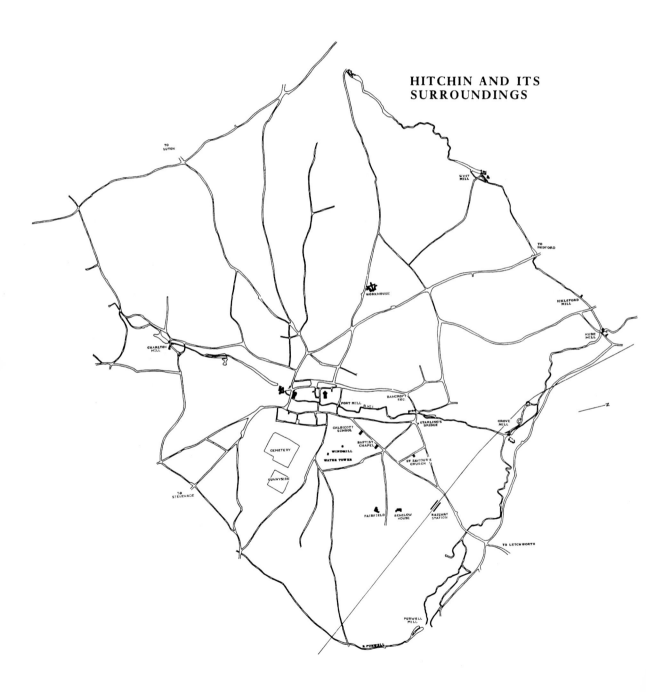

HITCHIN AND ITS
SURROUNDINGS

Index

References which relate to illustrations only are given in **bold**.

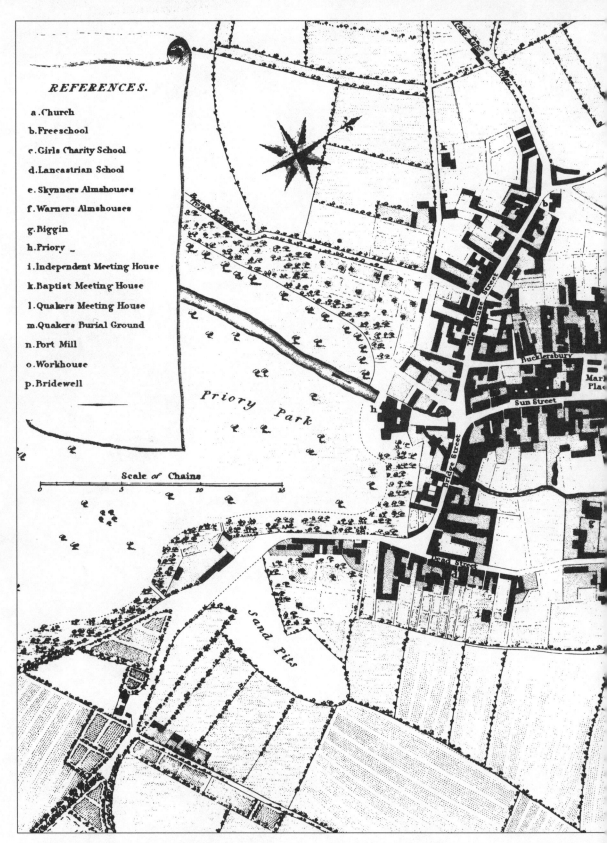

REFERENCES.

a. Church
b. Freeschool
c. Girls Charity School
d. Lancastrian School
e. Skynners Almshouses
f. Warners Almshouses
g. Biggin
h. Priory _
i. Independent Meeting House
k. Baptist Meeting House
l. Quakers Meeting House
m. Quakers Burial Ground
n. Port Mill
o. Workhouse
p. Bridewell

Scale of Chains

Priory Park

Sand Pits

Hitchin 1820, a privately published map, in the collections of Hitchin Museum.